LETTERS FROM FATHER

Also by MARGARET TRUMAN

Souvenir
Women of Courage
Harry S. Truman
Murder in the White House
Murder on Capitol Hill

MARGARET TRUMAN

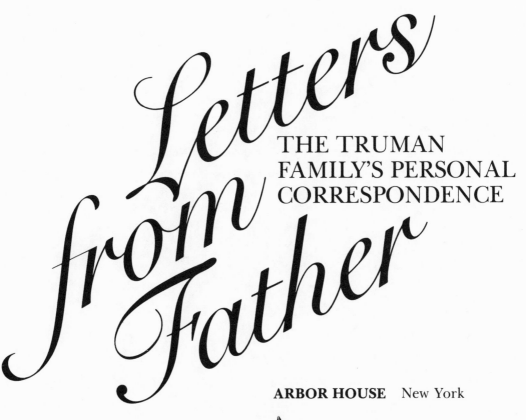

Letters from Father

THE TRUMAN FAMILY'S PERSONAL CORRESPONDENCE

ARBOR HOUSE New York

Library of Congress Catalog Card Number: 80-70224

ISBN: 0-87795-313-9

Design by Antler & Baldwin, Inc.
MANUFACTURED IN THE UNITED STATES OF AMERICA
10   9   8   7   6   5   4   3   2   1

For my mother,
Bess W. Truman

I would like to acknowledge the assistance of
Paulette Cooper.

CONTENTS

PREFACE

DAD first began to write me letters when I was seventeen years old. That was the year he started traveling extensively in his capacity as Chairman of the Senate Investigating Committee, which has come to be known as the Truman Committee.

The Truman Committee, established by the Senate to look into the defense program, was ultimately to put my father in a position of public prominence. Privately, however, it had the opposite effect. I began to see very little of him. Historians cite that period in my father's life as the real start of his lifelong political accomplishments. But whenever I think back to that period in my history, it represents the time that my father was always away.

We had always been close to each other from the time I was very young. Now, in my late teens, with him gone for long periods of time, I missed him intensely. And vice versa. The separation of those years was a difficult thing for both of us. So he tried to comfort himself, console me, and compensate for his absence by writing me some chatty letters.

Before that, whenever he had been away, he had carried on a continuing correspondence with my mother. I was included with a side remark, or a closing "kiss Margie for me." But now, he decided it was time to start a separate relationship by mail with his teenage daughter.

This decision also involved an obligation on my part. Dad made it clear, in almost every letter that he wrote me, that he expected me to do my share and write him back.

But all of his demands and entreaties were usually to no avail. Loving someone, and loving to write letters to someone, are two very different things. I was anxious to read, but never to write, and Dad frequently found himself sending his letters off into a vacuum.

This resulted in ceaseless lectures and justified accusations in his letters about his lazy daughter's non-letter-writing proclivities. A large number of his letters to me contain some comment concerning my lack of or grossly dilatory response to his epistles, and how anxiously he awaited a change in my habits. But nothing he wrote could persuade me to mend my ways. I simply did not like to write letters—and still consider it an odious chore to this day.

One might expect that he would have solved such a problem simply by calling me. The fact that he chose to write letters rather than use the telephone had nothing to do with a desire to put things down for posterity. When his correspondence with me started, the last thing he ever thought he would be one day was President of the United States of America. Even after he became President, I don't think any of his letters to me were written with a view to history. At the time that he wrote them, they were intended only for my eyes.

I believe Dad preferred to write rather than call because the telephone was not as much a part of his life as it is an integral part of our lives today. Remember that he was born in 1884. He was brought up at a time when telephones were not only a luxury, but an unsophisticated gadget that more often hindered than helped communication.

Dad liked to get his point across. He had learned when young that if you wanted to say something clearly to someone a distance away, and you wanted to hear what they had to say back, the best way was to sit down and write them a letter.

Besides which, with letters, there's the delightful anticipation of awaiting a response, and then lingering over the reply later. "If you knew how much I like to look at that scrawl of yours, you'd send one [a letter] oftener," he plaintively wrote me once.

My handwriting was a family joke, but it was not considered an acceptable excuse to avoid writing. Dad was glad for the opportunity to be able to read anything I would choose to scrawl back to him. "Of course, you inherit handwriting from both your mother and your dad that is individual and not very legible but I like to look at it anyway," he wrote me in 1955, still pleading for more responses from me, although a less persistent person would long since have given up hope. (Incidentally, my handwriting has always been somewhat illegible, since I had gone to two different schools. One taught me to print, the other trained me in the Spencer method, and I never did quite combine them correctly.)

The invariable and inevitable delays in my responses brought some very direct replies from him. "Is your arm paralyzed?" he once wrote me sarcastically. He also kept count of how often he had written me twice in a row without the obligatory (and rarely forthcoming) intervening letter back. On another occasion, in capital letters to ensure that his point would not be missed, he wrote me that "YOU OWE ME TWO LETTERS." He no doubt would have been delighted if I had taken that at all seriously.

But all of his demands, and pleas, even when they came from someone in so lofty a position as President of the United States, made little difference to his lazy daughter. I was content for him to pen his personal letters (which he usually wrote on formal stationery, including the pale green White House stationery) and for me to be able to reread each letter again and again.

I did not improve as his correspondent when I got older. In fact, letter writing became more burdensome for me after he became the President and I the President's daughter. Throughout those years, mail poured in to me from all over the world. I received letters from friends in my youth whom I had long since forgotten, from people I had only briefly met and barely knew, not to mention a multitude of missives from total strangers.

I knew that Dad would understand (or at least become accustomed to it by then) if I did not write him back. But I realized that most of these other correspondents would not be as tolerant or understanding. As a result, I had to answer literally hundreds of thousands of letters in those years—which did not make letter writing to Dad any less of a chore.

In addition to (reluctantly) answering all of that correspondence, in those days I also had to spend hundreds of hours on my homework. Then too, my musical activities and training took a great deal of my time. There was also a myriad of politically related functions and duties that a First Daughter must attend and attend to. Plus my regular social engagements with old friends and a steady array of new beaus.

Thus, Dad could wait. And wait he did. But Dad was not the type of person who liked to be put on the back burner by anyone, especially his daughter. "I am lonesome this morning," he wrote once, using a favorite ploy of his to try to get me to the writing table. "Thought maybe I might get a letter from my little girl. But I suppose she's busy with breathing exercises, vocal gymnastics and young gentlemen and so hasn't had the time."

Dad wrote these letters to alleviate his own loneliness as much as mine. Few people realize just how much the job of President of the United States is one of the most solitary positions in this world. This was especially true for Dad when Mother and I were away because the three of us were such a close family.

Even though he was surrounded by aides, servants

and Secret Service men, he was especially lonely and anxious to write and receive letters when Mother and I period-
ically left him to spend our summer in Independence. My
plane would not even have had the time to arrive in Missouri when he was already writing that "your pop has
missed you and your mama very much."

Such statements brought out mixed feelings on my
part. I was always happy to be departing Washington, and
returning to the simpler and more halcyon life in Independence, Missouri, where I was born and raised. But how
I hated to leave Dad. He invariably looked so forlorn
whenever he saw Mother and me go off that we were both
ready to immediately turn around and go back to him.

We knew that once we left him, he would often eat
alone, think about us, write to us, and wait for responses
that so rarely came from us. As busy as he was, he would
get up a little earlier in the morning so that he could
squeeze in a precious few moments to get some letters off
to his favorite women. "I was up at 4:00 A.M. so as to get a
letter to you, your ma and your Aunt Mary," he wrote on
July 19, 1947.

His letters, like him, were not at all pretentious. As in
his speeches, he tried to avoid pompous phraseology,
flowery language and "two dollar words"; he did not want
to give the person he was speaking to, or writing to, the
idea that he was trying to show off or show how important
he was. More importantly, "two dollar words" and pretentious phrases interfered with communicating facts, and
getting his point across was always uppermost in his mind.
When it came to deciding how to phrase something,
whether in a speech or a letter, his first rule was to make
everything as clear and understandable as possible.

Thus, the language of his letters is very much in
character with the way he spoke. As for their content, although he occasionally referred to the current events that
were so much a part of his life, as well as the country's, his

letters to me frequently showed more concern with the course of my life than with the course of history.

It was in his many joint letters to my mother and his sister, my Aunt Mary Jane Truman, that he frequently focused on current events and their historical antecedents. Unfortunately for history, however, most of these letters have been destroyed.

My Aunt Mary was uncomfortable about those letters because they included some family matters of a personal nature—although each also contained an invaluable and irreplaceable lesson for history. She could not adjust to the fact that any stranger could enter the Truman Library and read these letters (which had been donated by my mother). Aunt Mary considered these letters to be personal and for her and Mother's delectation alone.

She was friends with Dad's secretary and managed to inveigle her into giving her Dad's letters under some pretext. (Aunt Mary believed that these letters partially belonged to her, although in fact they belonged to my father.)

She then blithely burned them all. Fortunately, the contents of a few of them were saved, for I had gone through them earlier and quoted some in the biography I wrote of my father, *Harry S. Truman*.

Another group of letters from my father was also destroyed. These were the letters to my mother which he had written several years earlier. One Christmas, Dad came into the living room to find my mother systematically burning his letters.

"You shouldn't be doing that," he admonished her.

"Why not?" she asked him. "I've read them several times."

"But think of history," my father pleaded.

"I have," my mother said firmly.

When I was born, on February 17, 1924, I was christened Mary Margaret Truman. The Mary was after the same Aunt Mary Jane Truman, and Margaret was for my Grandmother Wallace. I never did like having two names, and still suspect that my father was responsible.

He was given the *S* for his middle initial after both of his grandfathers, each of whose names began with an *S*. In order not to insult by favoring either of them, it was always made a point in the family that the *S* in Dad's middle initial didn't stand for a thing. Perhaps he got so tired of not having a middle name (and having to explain that all the time to people) that he decided to compensate by burdening me with two names instead.

Dad called me "Marg" or "Margie" (both pronounced with a hard *G*) and I answered some of my letters to him with "Sistie," although I have no recollection now of why. All too often, however, Dad preferred to call me "Baby." I don't suppose I minded when I was three, but I was still objecting to this indignation—and to no avail—by the time I reached my late teens.

When I was seventeen, he wrote me that "You mustn't get aggravated when your old dad calls you his baby because he always will think of you as just that—no matter how old or how big you may get. When you'd cry at night, with that awful pain, he'd walk you and wish he could have it for you. When that little pump of yours insisted on going a hundred and twenty a minute when seventy would have been enough, he got a lot of grey hairs. And now—what a daughter he has! It is worth twice all the trouble and ten times the grey hairs."

Try to argue with that one—although I tried nonetheless. But there was just no way to stop him from this embarrassingly childish statement of endearment. Although I could tolerate it privately in his letters, it often made me uncomfortable when he continued to call me his "baby" in public, as was frequently the case.

I remember one time when I was about eighteen years

old and some politician came to talk with Dad in Independence. When I walked into the room later, the politician looked at me in such amazement that I asked him what the problem was.

"I can't believe it," he said. "Your father has been sitting here telling me about his baby for an hour. I expected a two-year-old toddler to come in."

Even that didn't stop Dad.

One habit Dad got into with me when I was young brought me pleasure rather than discomfiture. He was always slipping me money, first in person, and later in life by putting cash in his letters. The habit started when I was young and receiving an allowance of a dollar a week. I invariably immediately spent the entire sum on the movies, sometimes to see the same picture again and again.

My mother was a firm believer in teaching me to learn to live within a budget. Therefore, no matter how rapidly I ran out of money (which usually happened within a couple of days), she was adamant that I would have to wait until the following week in order to get more.

One evening I was teasing her for twenty-five cents to see a movie. Since I had already seen it, in fact spent my entire allowance on it, I was not getting a sympathetic hearing.

Mother was implacable, but Dad called me over and surreptitiously slipped me a quarter. We both thought our secret was safe, but as I bounded out of the house to see the movie, I could hear my mother saying "Harry, how am I ever going to teach this child the value of money if you won't cooperate with me?"

Mother didn't know anything about the money Dad was always slipping me in his letters (at least I don't think so). It was our little secret that Dad would give me money whenever the mood struck him—and I was glad in those days that the mood struck him so frequently, since after I was a child I stopped receiving a regular allowance.

At the bottom of many of his letters are mentions of these monetary gifts, and for those who are curious when they come across these references, the amount was usually twenty dollars. (Happily, when I was rereading these letters some years later, I found a twenty-dollar bill still tucked away in one of those letters which I had somehow missed!)

Another theme that runs throughout most of his letters concerned my singing. Music was always a very important and happy part of both of our lives. In fact, my first memory of my father had to do with music, although that was *not* a happy memory.

It was Christmas and, as usual, I was sick in bed with the flu. (I was frequently ill when I was a young child, especially, it seemed to me, at Christmas and on my birthdays.) The only thing I wanted then (other than to get out of that bed) was to get a set of electric trains.

Like my father, I was not the type of person to let others guess what was on my mind. For months, I made my desires known—loud and clear and often. The day before Christmas I was aware that there was a considerable amount of activity going on downstairs. I went to sleep that night confident that the next morning I would be playing with my dreamed-about electric trains.

Christmas morning, Dad came in to wake me up. "Wait until you see what I got you for Christmas," he said, barely able to contain his own excitement. He proudly carried me down into the parlor, and put me in front of . . . a shiny, brand-new baby grand piano.

I burst into tears and wouldn't go near it. Poor Dad. He was only earning a very modest salary at the time as presiding judge of the Jackson County Court. Furthermore, this occurred during the Depression. Buying a baby grand was practically tantamount to buying someone a Mercedes today.

To Dad, this piano was the most luxurious and generous gift on earth. While in retrospect I realize that it was, I didn't agree with him then. And, as I said earlier, like Dad, I was not the type to try to hide my feelings.

Eventually I relented, and Dad would even become my first piano teacher. We would also later occasionally play a few duets together, although Dad never accompanied me on the piano while I sang in private, as the press sometimes liked to imagine and report.

Nonetheless, I could never measure up to Dad as a pianist. He was a very talented amateur, more so than he has usually been given credit for. But I didn't even try to compete with him. While I enjoyed my early years on the piano, I derived more pleasure from singing in the choir (in Independence) and in glee clubs (in Washington). I began to devote more time to my voice than the keyboard and in my late teens started the long hard road to becoming a professional soprano.

Dad supported my aspirations for a musical career (he was way ahead on women's lib). However, he insisted that getting my college degree had to come before embarking on a career. His insistence that I finish my formal education first was probably based on the fact that his own education had been difficult for him to obtain and had frequently been interrupted. He did not want the same thing to happen to me.

Dad was also realistically aware of the inevitable complications of my being a President's daughter while trying to establish myself in my own right as a singer. This bothered him—and me.

People have hinted, sometimes subtly and often not so subtly, that after my father became President, I took opportunistic advantage of my circumstances and launched myself on a career to capitalize on the family name. Nothing could be further from the truth.

I have been stagestruck from my earliest days, and always was a natural-born ham. I would have pursued the stage—and a career in music was inevitable—no matter who my father was. What I discovered, as Dad feared, was that being a President's daughter in some ways made it harder for me than if I had simply been able to launch my career as Mary Margaret Truman, soprano.

Yes, because of my father, I was more easily able to obtain important engagements. But I also received more attention by first-string critics and more demanding audiences, who felt that because my father was the President, I had to be not better than the average but better than the best in order to justify my appearing on the stage.

Furthermore, for every critic who condoned or over-praised me because of my political position, others sought to find faults for the same reason. Thus, if they said good things, I had to wonder if they meant it; if they said bad things, I had to consider the source as well as the statement.

Dad, like all fathers, naturally only said good things. Many of his letters proudly discussed different aspects of my debut and career. As his only "baby," he would probably have backed me in whatever I did after I got my college degree. But deep down, like many fathers of a career woman, especially when she's an only child, there was one thing that Dad wanted even more than to see me be a singer.

He wanted to be a grandfather.

Even after I was established in my career, he would occasionally embarrass me by stating such things to reporters as "I'd rather have grandchildren in my family than a prima donna."

Not only my father, but also my mother, and especially the press, were anxious to get me married off, or at least engaged, while I was living in the White House. But I think I made a wise decision early in my White House residency that I would never marry until I left there.

Eventually, Dad did have his dream come true, and he

became the grandfather of four fine boys. My husband and I did not want them to be treated in any special way so we did not tell them when they were young exactly what role in history their grandfather had played.

When one of the boys came home from school one day, and asked if what he had heard from another child was true, I said "Yes. But that's not going to help you one bit in getting good grades. The only thing that's going to help you in school is if you do your homework."

In this way, the boys will be treated exactly the way their grandfather would have wished. Dad never wanted people to single him out and treat him with any greater deference because he was the Chief Executive. He realized that, at least initially, it had come about as an accident. And like all accidents, Dad had wanted to avoid this one.

Although he had spent much of his life in politics, starting out in that field long before I was born, the job of Vice-President was not an attractive one to him. It has been reported, and I have every reason to believe that it was true from his statements and letters to me, that when Dad was first asked by some of his political friends to run for Vice-President, he refused. "I talked it over with Bess," he is supposed to have said, "and we have decided against it. I've got a daughter and the limelight is no place for children."

Dad only agreed to take the position because Roosevelt personally asked him to. As a student of history, Dad had too much respect for the office, as well as the man who was then in it, to refuse a request coming from the Chief Executive.

After Dad became Vice-President of the United States, we continued to live in the same five-room apartment in Washington, D.C. on Connecticut Avenue, and our living standard remained exactly the same as before. I can remember only one improvement in my life-style and that was that the Vice-President was provided with a car and driver. As a result, I was driven to school each day. Prior to that, I had gone with friends or used public transportation.

Another change in my life, then, which was to become far more pronounced and troublesome when Dad became President, was a lack of privacy. Perhaps I was better able to endure this than some, because growing up in a small town (as Independence, Missouri, was in those days), in one way was not very different from living in the White House. Everybody knew your business.

Dad and Mother had the same privacy problems—much worse, of course—but they had other problems as well which may have made that one seem minor in comparison. Once Dad became Vice-President, his whole life changed radically. Besides the increased work load (perhaps a bigger problem for him than most Vice-Presidents because the President was dying, although we were as unaware of that then as was the rest of the country), he was plunged into a nonstop social whirl which he had tried to avoid whenever possible during his earlier public career.

But now, under an ailing President, there was no way for him to maintain a private and nonpolitical social life any longer. Dad recognized that someone as important to the people as a Vice-President had an obligation to meet as many of the people as possible. Mother, who had always considered politics to be an unpleasant chore that had to be taken care of, went along with Dad in whatever he wanted.

When Roosevelt died, Dad never allowed becoming the President of the United States to overwhelm him. He maintained the same attitude toward most things that he had had before.

For example, although Dad had the proper respect for the historical significance of the White House, and what the awesome edifice represented, he treated the place in some ways the same as our house in Independence, Missouri.

Dad was always going around at night checking the windows and doors in the White House to make sure they were properly locked up. His solicitousness paid off. One time, when Mother and I were out of town, Washington was struck in the middle of the night by a rainstorm which rapidly reached hurricane proportions.

Dad, wearing his striped pajamas and probably still in his bare feet, got out of bed to check whether it was raining in. It was—pouring in through the windows in buckets.

Dad sprinted to his bathroom, grabbed a load of towels, and went from room to room of the White House, mopping up the rain that was cascading in. He continued to do this for about a half an hour until one of the ushers, attracted by the noise and lights, came to investigate what was happening. Only then did he receive assistance. It had simply never occurred to Dad earlier to call out to anyone for help, any more than he would have sought assistance had the same thing happened in our home in Missouri.

Basically, he was the same person as he had been before. I certainly never really thought about him very much as being the President. To me, he was just Dad. I'll admit that initially, however, I was a little impressed with my new status.

Occasionally, at the beginning, I did try to stretch things a little to see how far I could go. But when that happened, my father was quick to remind me that I was the recipient of a public responsibility. My mother also wasted no time in reminding me that she had brought me up to be a lady. And both were quick to emphasize that my main objective was to finish college and get on with my music.

Just as Dad did not really change when he became President, his letters from that period were as forthright and affectionate as his earlier ones. One generally has to look to the date of the letter rather than to its tone or content to recognize that this momentous change in his life had taken place.

Although written communications with Dad did not change when he went from the Vice-Presidency to the top position, when I saw him in person, I did try to interrupt him less with trivial matters. Obviously, he had a lot more on his mind, especially since those years were particularly precarious and tumultuous times.

But as a family, we still tried to get together as frequently as we had before. For example, we all still made a point of having breakfast together. Actually, that was a disappointment to me, since the one luxury of living in the White House that I really would have liked would have been to have daily (or even occasional) breakfasts in bed. But my mother soon took care of that daydream, and made it clear that there would be no breakfast in bed for me except when I was sick.

In addition to breakfasts, when there were no official luncheons that Dad, Mother, or I had to attend, Dad would leave the executive wing and come over to have lunch with us each day, and when possible, also dinner.

Afterwards, in the evenings, Dad would usually go off to make a speech somewhere (if he wasn't out of town on official business), or work late on some important matters at the executive wing. Mother was frequently attending some official function, and I guess I was the luckiest one because I was often out at a party.

On those rare occasions when there wasn't something we had to do, we all sat around in the private upstairs lounge just like any other family. Dad and Mother were likely to be reading, or carrying on the casual conversation common to husbands and wives who have been happily married for years.

They would fill each other in on news about our many relatives and old friends; I was likely to talk about school,

singing, or what my friends were up to. Since they were
interested in my social life, I often tantalized them with
tidbits about my new beau, or just filled them in on what I
was planning to do the next day.

We rarely dealt in gossip about public figures and
political personalities. If I expressed an unkind opinion of
someone, as many young people are wont to do, I was
summarily silenced. Neither of my parents were mean
about people and tried to teach me to be the same way.

We also did not discuss politics that much. While such
conversations probably cropped up more frequently in
person than they did in Dad's letters to me, it was definitely
not the main topic of conversation. Dad was inundated
with the country's—and the world's—problems for almost
eight years, many more if you include the time that he was
Senator and Vice-President. In his rare leisure time, there
were more relaxing and pleasant things for him to focus
on with his family.

This dearth of discussions about political matters
seems to surprise some, since some people have a very
curious notion about what a President's family discusses.
Since the President's decisions go down in history, they
seem to think that historical circumstances surround the
making of those decisions.

Thus, some picture the President as gathering his
family around him, and in hushed tones, asking for their
opinions and weighing all the options with them before
coming to a world-changing conclusion. Besides the fact
that a President's family is not his Cabinet, I don't think
the President of a major corporation consults his wife and
children before making a major decision either. Although
I had some inkling—and sometimes even knowledge—of
certain things in advance, there were others that I learned
first from the media just like everyone else in this country.

The most comprehensive description of the changes
in my life when Dad became the President was the one that
I wrote in my autobiography, *Souvenir*:

"I began to be bidden to stand in the receiving lines of embassy receptions, to attend dinners where my partners ranged from a General of all the armies to atomic scientists, to go to balls where I was swung out by the presidents of foreign powers, princes, prime ministers, and movie stars. I became the recipient of fabulous gifts, and people named hats, colors and flowers after me. Musicians composed scores and lyricists wrote words that were for me alone. A convertible was provided for my personal use at the White House and I began to get hundreds of letters containing advice, suggestions that I browbeat my father into doing something, and proposals of marriage. I had regiments of beaus, who squired me hither and yon and made me pretty speeches. I was invited to christen boats, planes and products, and to attend race meets, hunts, cruises, cotillions, fairs, breakfasts, lunches, teas, cocktail parties, dinners, and receptions. I rode in private cars, private limousines, private yachts, and private planes but had no privacy."

When I left the White House, I continued my singing career, went on to do some summer stock, a lot of radio and television broadcasting work, then comedy acting, and now I spend most of my time as a wife, mother, and at another career: writing.

I find it somewhat ironic that someone who had the President of the United States begging her for years to write him something, *and* to no avail, should have ultimately voluntarily chosen to spend her time putting pen to paper.

This second career may have developed in self-defense. I wrote the first of my six books, my autobiography, when I heard that someone else was planning to write a book about my life. I decided that I was the one who should really do it, and did. Maybe I was still trying to please my father, though, and fulfill his prophecy. He wrote me at the end of 1946 that "you write interestingly and perhaps when you arrive [at a certain age] and your good voice cracks you can become a great storywriter."

Dad would have enjoyed my two current mystery novels (*Murder in the White House* and *Murder on Capitol Hill*) because mystery—and history—were his favorite reading matter. I shall always remember Dad and Mother at the end of a difficult day relaxing by passing mystery stories around to each other. (Mother also liked to read the sports pages of newspapers.)

I am glad now that I also shared another habit of Dad's of never wanting to throw things away. I kept his letters, even those I received when quite young, throughout all of these years. I'll admit, however, that I was quite casual about them, keeping them tucked away in an unlocked desk drawer in my apartment. (When this book is published, I plan to donate them to the Truman Library.) To me, they were letters from Dad, not letters from a President of the United States of America.

Most of these letters have never been seen by the public before, and they show a personal side of my father not contained in his historical notes and memoranda.

His letters also show him to be not only an extraordinary President, but also an extraordinary human being with exemplary beliefs and unimpeachable values. They show the warm human side of a man burdened with the most pressing problems in this world but never too busy or too preoccupied to take time out for the second great love of his life, his daughter.

While I was rereading his letters to compile this book, I couldn't help but think how lucky I was—not so much to have been the daughter of the President of the United States as simply to have been his daughter.

Harry S. Truman to Margaret Truman

Pre-Presidential Years (1934-44)

Mother and Dad's Wedding picture. I remember playing with the shoes.

When I received my first letter from Dad, I was ten years old,
and he was on his way to Washington

ABOARD THE NATIONAL LTD. TO INDEPENDENCE, MO.

Sunday Dec. 31, '34

My Dear Little Girl:—

I am again on the Baltimore and Ohio going to the City
of George Washington. I hope that at this time next year,
you and mother will be on the same fine train making the
same trip for a six months' stay. We have just left
Vincennes, Indiana. You remember how the Wabash River
was all over the road there when we were going home from
the South.

There are two little girls on the train one about four
and the other six. They have red plaid skirts and yellow
waists just alike so they must be sisters. The younger one
is always finding something new in the observation car
to cry out about and show surprise over. They have a big
sister with them who spends her time saying: "sh- sh- don't
make so much noise." There are three Annapolis boys in
uniform who enjoy the kids a lot but I am inclined to think
that an old maid (I guess she's one) is somewhat annoyed
at them. The six year old has her hair bobbed just like yours
but the smaller one has pig tail plaits just like Aunt Mary
Jane used to wear. But I'll bet she's looking forward to the
day when she can have her hair bobbed don't you?

I hope you are entirely well and are doing a lot of
bicycle riding by this time. You should have all your
Christmas books read by this time though I'd think.

Has mother been a good girl? I hope she has and that
you haven't had to be spanked.

I'll send her a telegram from New York tomorrow and
maybe write her a letter. You give her a good kiss for me.

Your loving
Daddy

In 1941, when he decided to start corresponding with me. I was expected to write the first letter.

TO WASHINGTON, D.C. (POSTCARD)—POSTMARKED 27? SEPTEMBER 1941

Where is that letter I was to have here? Too much school? Maybe. I'm still looking.

Dad

*In 1941, our regular correspondence began. This is his first
real letter to me, and he started off with a lesson in history.*

SPRINGFIELD, MO. TO WASHINGTON, D.C.

October 1, 1941

My dear Margie:—

Your nice letter came yesterday to the Melbourne Hotel
in St. Louis. I am glad you like your Spanish and your
teacher of it. In days to come it will be a most useful asset.
Keep it up and when we get to the point where we can take
our South American tour you can act as a guide and
interpreter.

Ancient History is one of the most interesting of all
studies. By it you find out why a lot of things happen today.
But you must study it on the basis of the biographies of the
men and women who lived it. For instance, if you were
listening in on the Senate Committee hearings of your dad,
you'd understand why old Diogenes carried a lantern in the
daytime in his search for an honest man. Most everybody is
fundamentally honest, but when men—or women are
entrusted with public funds or trust estates of other people
they find it most difficult to honestly administer them. I
can't understand or find out why that is so—but it is.

You will also find out that people did the same things,
made the same mistakes and followed the same trends as
we do today. For instance, the Hebrews had a republic three
or four thousand years ago that was almost ideal in its
practical workings. Yet they tired of it and went to a
monarchy or totalitarian state. So did Greece, Carthage,
Rome.

Israel had its David and Solomon, Greece, Alexander
the Great, Carthage, its Hannibal and Rome, Julius Caesar. I
wish you'd take Mr. Plutarch and read very carefully his
history of various Greek and Roman heroes.

Hannibal was the greatest of all military leaders. We have only the records of his enemies to judge him by. But he won every battle for twenty-one years in the enemy's country and lost the war. All studies of military tactics are based on his campaigns. Alexander the Great inaugurated the present-day blitz and panzer program. Read about his phalanx and how he used it. Hitler evidently has read about them—as had Napoleon and Robert E. Lee. I'm glad you like Ancient History—wish I could study it again with you. Buy this month's National Geographic and see how like us Ancient Egypt was. Here is a dollar to buy it with. You can buy soda pop with the change.

You tell your old grandmother how sorry I am to be away from home while she is there—but I really can't help it.

Hope you had a good time at your luncheon-show. Kiss mamma + say hello to grandmother. Lots of love to you.

XXXXXXXXX   Dad
OOOOOOOO

I had been very sickly as a child, and Dad and I hoped that was all behind me.

NASHVILLE, TENN. TO WASHINGTON, D.C.

October 5, 1941

Dear Margie:—

I have a hotel radio in my room. Have been listening to Fred Mirnn[?] et al. It was a nice program. The co-ed singing program is now on, and the charming young lady who is the "charming co-ed" hasn't half the voice of my baby.

You mustn't get aggravated when your old dad calls you his baby, because he always will think of you as just that—no matter how old or how big you may get. When you'd cry at night with that awful pain, he'd walk you and wish he could have it for you. When that little pump of yours insisted on going a hundred and twenty a minute when seventy would have been enough, he got a lot of grey hairs. And now—what a daughter he has! It is worth twice all the trouble and ten times the grey hairs.

Miss Estelle Remy[?] has just sung for $100. A nice girl—a nice voice but still I'm prejudiced you see. Went to the Baptist Church in Caruthersville this morning and the good old Democratic preacher spread himself. He preached to me and at me and really settled the whole foreign situation but it won't work. Had a nice time anyway and then had dinner with all the politicians in Southeast Mo.—and they really settled the Senior Senator.

Last week I had dinner in Trenton and the Chinese Consul General at Chicago was on the program with me and he made a corking speech to the United States Senator present and not to the audience at all. It's awful what it means to some people to meet a Senator. You'd think I was Cicero or Cato. But I'm not. Just a country jake who works at the job.

Now you be a nice girl and win some more prizes so I can brag some more when some of these snoots try to high hat. Lots of love, kiss mamma for me.

XXXXXXXXXXX   Dad
OOOOOOOOOO

The picture of Mother which Dad carried
to France in World War I.

This is an example of one of many history lessons that he gave me. You can also see his Southern prejudice here.

ROANOKE, VA. TO WASHINGTON, D.C.

Monday, Nov. 10, '41

Dear Margie:—

Here is a classic. I wonder if it is true. Maybe you can tell me.

It was a pleasure to get a chance to talk with your mother and you just now. That's an American colloquialism, "just now." It really means nothing. But we make it mean, "immediate past time."

Yesterday I drove over the route that the last of the Confederate Army followed before the surrender. I thought of the heartache of one of the world's great men on the occasion of that surrender. I am not sorry he did surrender but I feel as your old country grandmother has expressed it—"What a pity a white man like Lee had to surrender to old Grant." She'd emphasize the white and the old. That "old" had all the epithets a soldier knows in it. But Grant wasn't so bad. When old Thad Stevens wanted to send Lee to jail, Grant told him he'd go too. If Grant had been satisfied like General Pershing to rest on his military honors and hadn't gone into politics he'd have been one of the country's great.

But Marse[?] Robert was one of the world's great. He and Stonewall rank with Alexander, Hannibal and Napoleon as military leaders—and Lee was a good man along with it.

    Kiss mama and lots for you   Dad
XXXXXXXXXXXX

The "Washington Merry-Go-Round" was Drew Pearson.
Dad was pleasantly surprised that he wrote something true
for a change.

MEMPHIS, TENN. TO WASHINGTON, D.C.

November 16, 1941

My dear Margie:—

I wanted to say my dear baby, and then I thought what a grand young lady I have for a daughter—and I didn't. You made your papa very happy when you told him you couldn't be bribed. You keep that point of view and I'll always be as proud of you as I always want to be. Anyone who will give up a principle for a price is no better than John L. Lewis or any other racketeer—and that's what John L. is. Your dad won the brass ring in the "Washington Merry-Go-Round" day before yesterday. Why? Because the two liars who write it said that publicity means not so much to him. It doesn't but they don't believe it.

I am hoping I still get the nice letter. There is one awful three days ahead. I'm going to have to show up graft and misuse of gov't funds. It will hurt somebody—maybe the one who doesn't deserve it. But your dad has gotten himself into a job that has to be done and no matter who it hurts it will be.

Here's something for you.

Kiss mamma for me.

Lots of love   OOOO

          Dad

XXXXXXXXXXXX

OOOOOOOOOO

*Dad was doing a lot of traveling as part of his work on the
Senate Investigating Committee (the Truman Committee).*

They found out who I am at the Ft. Sumter and I had to
move

Saturday

Dear Margie:—

Here are some picture cards (enclosed) of Charleston
—you must make the a very broad and roll the r to get the
fullest effect.

The town is laid out like Baltimore. The streets just
came about as place to walk and lead a cow. None of 'em
except the boulevards around the bay over 20 feet wide.
Wish you + your ma were along.

XXXXXXX Dad OOOO
OOOOOOOO

*This letter, appraising my assets, was written by Dad from
Los Angeles while he was touring some California Defense
Plants.*

ABOARD THE SANTA FE CHIEF TO WASHINGTON, D.C.

Friday, Mar. 13, 1942
Los Angeles to Albuquerque

Dear Margie:— Your old dad was sorely disappointed when
he found no letter awaiting him at the St. Francis Hotel in
San Francisco. There was one from your mother and two
from Aunt Mary—but none from Margie. You see the
number averaged out all right. I'd expected three letters
and I had three but not from three people.

You are now a young lady eighteen years young and
you are responsible from now on for what Margie does.
Your very excellent and efficient mother has done her duty
for eighteen years. Your dad has looked on her and has been
satisfied with the result.

You have a good mind, a beautiful physique and a
possible successful future outlook—but that now is up to
you. You are the mistress of your future. All your mother
and dad can do is to look on, advise when asked, and hope
and wish you a happy one. There'll be troubles and sorrow a
plenty but there'll also be happy days and hard work.

From a financial standpoint your father has not been a
shining success but he has tried to leave you something
that (as Mr. Shakespeare says) cannot be stolen—an
honorable reputation and a good name. You must continue
that heritage and see that it isn't spoiled. You're all we have
and we both count on you.

I've had a pleasant and restful trip. Met a young
Captain in San Francisco who told me his name is Truman
Young. He is a great-grandson of the famous Brigham. I
delivered Mr. Vaughan at Ft. Mason and we hated to part.
The general gave me his plane + I flew to L.A. Will see Sen.
Hatch tomorrow and you on Monday. Kiss your mamma for
me + lots of love to you   XXX
XXXXXXXXXXXX Dad
OOOOOOOOO

*Dad had just made a speech for young people. He always
liked doing that and was very good at it.*

HOT SPRINGS, VA. TO WASHINGTON, D.C.

May 2, 1942

Dear Margie:— Your old dad was very much gratified this
morning when he went to the desk to get a letter from you
which had been forwarded from No'th Ca'lina. It was a nice
letter. When your mamma told me you'd made the honor
roll again I didn't feel quite so badly about not getting a
letter. I'm very proud of you—as I most always am.

Had a letter from Aunt Mary saying that your country
grandmother had received one from you and that it had
made her very happy. That makes me happy too. You know
she can do so little now except listen to the radio.

You should have been with me at the meeting in Chapel
Hill. When I finished the speech those smart young men
and women began firing questions at me on every phase of
the war and the government. It was a very warm spot and I
could have used a bright young lady helper by the name of
Margaret. They were kind enough afterwards to say they
enjoyed it. Well I did too.

Hope you and your ma and me may be able to visit this
place sometime together. It is very beautiful. But there's
arrangements only for sporty people. Your pap can only
walk and sleep.

Kiss your mother for me. Lots of love and kisses to you.
XXXXX   Dad   OOO
XXXXX   OOO

Although Dad didn't like movies, he did like live shows—
especially vaudeville. Here, he reminisces and gives me a
short course in the history of Kansas City Theater.

WASHINGTON, D.C. TO INDEPENDENCE, MO.

Read my proposed speech I sent your mother about draft
dodgers.

Washington, D.C.
June 23, 1942

My dear Daughter,

It was a nice belt and a good letter. The belt fits and
matches every suit I have. I'll wear it a long, long time I
hope. It must have been rather embarrassing to have that
horn in operation on a continuing basis. Maybe most people
thought you were taking a bride and groom to the train.
That's the way the Italians in Kansas City celebrate a
wedding.

You'll never believe it but your dad went to a picture
show all by himself last Saturday but I've forgotten what it
was. I know it was rather silly + I did not see it all. The
news part was good. It showed the sinking of all our
battleships at Pearl Harbor. Showed the Arizona blowing
up and several others sinking. They also had a good old-
fashioned vaudeville show like your dad used to see
when he was your age some forty years ago. I wish they'd
never have closed the old Orpheums. I saw many famous
actors at ours in Kansas City when it was over on West 9th
Street. I saw Sarah Bernhardt there, and Chick Sale, Eva
Tanguay and John Drew. The Four Cohans and other
famous musical shows used to come to the old Grand at
Seventh and Walnut when your dad worked in a bank and
acted as an usher at night. I saw Pinafore, Florodora, the
Bohemian Girl, Williams and Walker famous negro actors,
Jim Corbett and a lot of others you've read about.

Your mamma + me used to go to the Willis Wood at 11th + Baltimore to hear Valdimer De Pachman play Mozart's 9th Sonata, and see Henry Irving and Ellen Terry play Julius Caesar and Othello, Richard Mansfield play King Richard III and Dr. Jekel [sic] and Mr. Hyde—and then be afraid to go home. Actors had to have voices in those days because there was no mike. Hope you are having a nice summer. We have a new piano. It's bigger and better looking than the old one.

The girls say hello. Kiss mamma for me. Lots of love

XXXXXXXXX   Dad   XXXXX
XXXXXXXX   OOOO

The house in Independence, Missouri—*before* the fence.

*Even at this early date, Dad's taking a crack at General
MacArthur. Dad felt that he should have stayed with his
men.*

WASHINGTON, D.C. TO INDEPENDENCE, MO.

Washington, D.C.
June 30, 1942

Dear Margie:— It was a treat to have your very hurried
letter yesterday. It is now very early in the morning of the
day before Mr. Canfil[?] and I start to Missouri. That is if we
can get the necessary gas to make it. There has been a real
gas famine. All the gas stations have signs out "No Gas
Today."

But some cars seem to run anyhow and some just stop
alongside the street. Guess we <u>are</u> in a war at last. Your dad
has been in one for a year and a half and I suppose will be
for another year or so. General Wilson from Australia called
me up last night and will be in to see me at 7:30. I guess he
can tell me all about the war in the Far East and Down
Under. I'm not very fond of MacArthur. If he'd been a
real hero he'd have gone down with the ship + hoped for a
transfer when prisoners were exchanged. Mr. Shields will
leave Shanghai today for Porto Lourenço in Portuguese
East Africa and will be home about Sept. 1. I have that
officially. Intended to wire Mrs. Shields but didn't for fear
that there might be a slip up as there is so many times.

I'm glad the horn is behaving and I hope its operator is
too. It has been a most dull and lonesome June for me. Get
up at 5:30 drink tomato juice and milk, go to work, eat some
toast and orange juice and work some more, maybe have a
committee fight + a floor fight go to bed + start over. Kiss
mamma hope everybody is well. Lots of love

XXXXXXXXXXXXXXXX Dad OOOOO
    OOOOO

*Dad was all by himself and feeling lonely because Mother
and I went to Missouri. (He even missed my not turning up
the radio so loudly it always sounded as if the concert was
right in the house. That used to drive him up the wall.)*

WASHINGTON, D.C. TO INDEPENDENCE, MO.

Washington, D.C.
June 16, 1943

Dear Margie:— It was certainly nice to find your good letter
on my desk when I came in this morning. I'm very, very
lonesome without you and your mother. The apartment is a
dreary place when there's no one to run the radio and put to
bed.

Glad you and Dan had a ride, I hope the flood isn't too
bad. Don't worry about your singing just get up there and do
it like you were in the parlor at home and no one listening.
You have a lovely voice and I like to listen to it, so don't let
anyone spoil it by putting frills into it. Sing like a bird—just
as the Almighty intended you to.

I found lots of mail, most of it from soldiers and
chistlers [sic] who want jobs. There have been lots of
customers who just wanted to talk. Leighton Shields has
been in both days. So has Mr. Duncan.

Wish you'd have been with me to see Mr. Phillips'
museum of American art. He has Indian pottery, blankets
and crude pictures that date back as far 2,000 years and he
also has a collection of beautiful paintings of the West that
are unequaled anywhere. On the ranch he has buffalo, elk,
llamas, gnus, peafowls, parrots and most every kind of bird.
So it was a good visit. Be sure and write to me when you can.
Lots of love + kiss mamma for me.

XXXXXXXX   Dad   X
OOOOOOOOOOOO

*I gave him a picture for Father's Day and he was very
pleased with it.*

WASHINGTON, D.C. TO INDEPENDENCE, MO.

Washington, D.C.
June 20, '43

My dear Daughter:—

I appreciated the Dad's day remembrance very much.
Didn't even know it was such a day. Found it sticking under
the door when I started down here a while ago. Those barns
do look like Ohio red barns. Wish we could see them again—
but we probably will wait a long time.

Sent you the magazines and funnies out of the
Washington papers, also a clipping from last night's <u>Star</u>
showing your pa crowning the Queen of the Night of
Thrills. They had an excellent show but I only stayed until
nine o'clock and then got them to take me home. Had dinner
with Ed M. Kim and Mrs. Ed last night, also young Ed and
a young lady marine and two other young marine lieuts.
and their young lady friends. One of the young ladies is
the daughter of former Gov. Cochrane of Nebraska. She is
a lovely child—guess she wouldn't appreciate being called a
child as she just graduated from the University of Nebraska.

Had lunch with Mr. + Mrs. Strickler at the Mayflower
yesterday and she said some nice things about your voice. I
knew that already but it was nice for her to say it.

Kiss Mamma   Love to you   X

OOOOO   Dad
XXXXXXXX

*Dad was angry because the postmaster didn't take in my
Grandmother Truman's mail to her. She was nearly ninety,
and he didn't think she should have to go out and get her own
mail then.*

WASHINGTON, D.C. TO INDEPENDENCE, MO.

Washington, D.C.
June 25, 1943

My dear Margie:—

It was nice to have a letter from you and two from your
mamma today. Had one from Aunt Mary too. I hope you and
your mother can go out to see my mamma before you leave.
It must be rather lonesome for her when she knows
everybody's so far away. I sent her a special delivery letter a
few days ago and that good for nothing postmaster woman
didn't even take her the papers, but some little boy came by
and got them for her. You can't understand how anybody
could be as selfish and unthoughtful. Mary used to take the
mail to her mother all the time when she was away on her
vacation. My old Grandpa Young told me that a scrub never
outgrew his parentage and the white trash would remain
just that no matter how much money and education they
obtained. I used to doubt it but I fear the old man was more
nearly right than I.

That flood must have been terrible. I feel as badly as
you do over those potatoes and the effects on the poor
farmers. But it's just like bombs and tornadoes. We just have
to take it and make the best of it.

I am enclosing you a note which I want you to give to
your mamma on the train after you get to Kansas City. Now
remember after you get to K.C., send me Fred's address, I
haven't got it and I can't write until I get it.

Kiss your mamma when you get this and <u>twice</u> on
Monday night. My best to your grandmother. Lots of love

Dad

I was out in Denver with my aunt and uncle and was singing in the chorus—as the 364th of 365 gypsies.

WASHINGTON, D.C. TO DENVER, COLO.

July 11, 1943

My dear Daughter:—

Nice to get your good letter of last Wednesday. Yes I stayed at the Palmer House in a bedroom-and-parlor suite. Also saw the show one night with the same orchestra leader as when we were there. Had breakfast every morning at the Morrison Coffee Shop. Our man ran second, but that means he may be elected at the next session. They used your dad as a drawing card and a show horse to get the customers in.

I sure wish I could see you and hear you in that opera but I can't. Talked to your mamma this morning and she said you would be singing this week only and I can't leave here before Thursday or Friday and it will take me until Monday or Tuesday of next week to get there, then I'll have to stay at home until I can see all the family and get a reservation. So I expect it will be Friday after next before I arrive. Be sure and send me that write-up and picture. I am very proud of you so don't let me down.

I'm hoping to stay in Denver with you four or five days and come home with you. Hope it isn't as hot there as it is here. It is at least 92° and damp. Had roast beef with Joe Guffey a few minutes ago. Your Uncle Vivian is here. He'll go home tomorrow. Kiss your mamma for me. Lots of love to you.

Dad

*On my twentieth birthday, he gave me some advice and
predicted my future for me.*

JACKSONVILLE, FLA. TO WASHINGTON, D.C.

                                        Jacksonville, Fla.
                                        February 15, 1944

My dear Daughter:—

On Thursday, the day after tomorrow, you'll be twenty
years old. It doesn't seem possible but the facts of time make
it so. I hope that you have a most happy birthday and that
you'll have an unlimited number of them in the future. That,
of course, will depend upon you and circumstances. You
first and then what happens as old father time unreels the
future. You must meet contingencies as they arrive and face
them squarely. You should have enough of your mother's
willpower and strength of character and your dad's
affability to make out.

When you finish that education you are after and
become the great singer I'm sure you can, then remember
that on your 20th birthday your dad foretold it.

Florida, as represented by Jacksonville, is one heck of a
place. The sun was shining brightly when I arrived Sunday,
but it turned cold in the night and clouded up, then Monday
it got warm and Monday night it stormed and rained and
blew a gale, breaking windows and keeping the customers
away from my speech. They wouldn't have come anyway,
but they had an excuse. There were about 200 and they were
kind and enthusiastic.

The optimistic national committee man and committee
woman had assured me there'd be 2,000—but zeros are easy
to erase or put on in politics.

Anyway I hope you have a happy birthday. Kiss your
mother for me and say hello to grandma.

I'm leaving for Tampa this morning.

Lots of love + good wishes.

                                        Dad

Dad wrote this letter to me the day after his sixtieth birthday.

KANSAS CITY, MO. TO ?

May 9, 1944

My dear Daughter:—

The book was just what I wanted. I've been reading it
ever since it came. It will be very helpful in answering
political lies in this campaign.

I am so glad you made that good grade in your botany
exam. I'm prouder of you every day. I always have more to
brag about than Snyder or Jim Pendergast when I see them
and we talk daughters.

Glad you got in a music lesson and hope you had a nice
time at all your weddings.

I spoke to the cadets at Kemper last night on the 100th
birthday of the school and my own 60th. They gave me a
beautiful cake with six candles on it—one for each ten
years. Four of the boys presented it and then I cut it and
gave each of them a piece of it and a piece to each one at the
head table. One of the four was the son of Martin Dies of
Texas. They gave me quite an ovation after my talk.

I'm surely lonesome to see you. Here is some allowance
money. I expect you are in debt. Lots of love.

Dad

In the second half of this letter, he seemed to both sense and recoil from the destiny that was awaiting him.

HOT SPRINGS NATIONAL PARK, ARK. TO WASHINGTON, D.C.

May 13, 1944

My dear Daughter:—

I am sitting here all alone in a great big suite in this hotel for rich [?] listening to the Boston Symphony over the Little Rock + Hot Springs Radio. Of course I thought of my sweet and pretty daughter when I turned on the good music. A Mr. Tomlinson had given a news broadcast from Recife, Brazil before the symphony came on. He had a couple of sailors to help him, one of whom had been in Brazil for two years and ten months. This sailor told how he'd been taken into all the exclusive clubs, been wined and dined by the populace—but that now too many North Americans were in town and of course were not such a novelty. That was true in France in 1917–18—no doubt was true in England, in Australia, in Africa and wherever else we've sent troops.

We all get used to things and take them for granted. The other boy was a twenty-two year old who was in a religious mood. He was telling about the men in Recife trying to find a consolation from Matthew V, VI, + VII and some other things. And then the Symphony came on and the sponsor had three specially decorated sergeants as guests who had been over the various fronts, New Guinea, Italy and Germany. All had special decorations and were not happy to make speeches. No good soldier is a speech maker or a showman. That's why we don't like Dugout[?] Douglas from Australia. That Symphony is playing the Butterfly I used to try to play. Sometimes your dad wishes he'd gone on and been a music hall pianist or a bank vice-president. You see Isenhour's [sic] brother started in the National Bank of Commerce after your pa did an is now its executive vice-president—and he didn't know how to turn on a gas jet when he came to Kansas City—asked old Mrs. Trow our boarding housekeeper for a coal oil lamp. But that's not to his discredit. It just shows how great is opportunity in good old U.S.A. And it is greater now than ever. If I didn't believe I'd lived in the greatest age in history I'd wish to live in yours, but I'd want your mother and you to live with me.

Your old dad would be very, very happy if his daughter would always have a letter waiting for him when he gets to a new place.

You are all he has for the future and you of course cannot appreciate what you mean to him.

Kiss mamma—twice for me. Tell grandmother hello for me and loads of love for yourself.

Dad

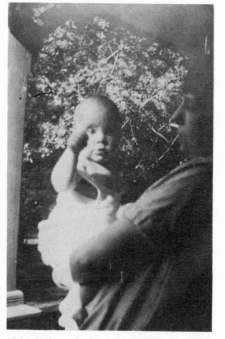

Me—already laying down the law.

*Obviously, Dad did not think much of Dewey, which should
come as no surprise to anyone.*

WASHINGTON, D.C. TO DENVER, COLO.

Monday
July 3, 1944

Dear Margie:— Here are some letters and a telegram to
your mother. They were out at the house along with a lot of
bills etc.

It was nice to talk to you yesterday. I spent most of the
day in bed. I bought a <u>Star</u>, <u>Post</u>, <u>Times-Herald</u> and a <u>New
York Times</u> and went to sleep over each one.

They're sure trying hard to make a man of little Dewey.
It's going to be rather hard to do.

Kiss your mamma. Tell grandmother and Fred +
Christie + the kids hello.

Lots of love, Dad.

Here, he's describing his work on the Senate Investigating Committee (the Truman Committee) which took up so much of his time and interest.

Washington,
July 4, 1944

Dear Daughter:— It was a very nice letter and your dad was very glad to get it. Hope you had a nice time at your late party and the swimming party. I guess I should have stayed in Colorado. It seems to be a gay place.

Mr. Wallgren came down to see me yesterday and brought three beautiful tablespoons for serving. They are whoppers—bigger than any we have. They belong to the new set. He had a fat old man with him by the name of Macnider. He's a cousin of the famous Hanford who was national commander of the Legion, Asst. Sec. of War under the Republicans and is now Minister or something down in the South Pacific.

This Bill Macnider is a partner of Mr. McBoyle who owns the second richest gold mine in the world at Grass Valley, Calif.

We all went to see Mr. McBoyle when we were in San Francisco. He lives in the most gorgeous apartment I ever saw. It made the Stewarts' look like ours beside the Stewarts'. It had white velvet carpets on the floor with grand oriental rugs on top, paintings and furniture to match. And to set it all off, Mrs. McBoyle, a real redheaded, blue-eyed Irish woman about fifty like you read about in story books. She spent most of her time crying while we were there because she thought he would die any minute—but he's up and getting well.

He and Macnider[?] think that this Special Committee of mine is the biggest thing in the government because we cut a lot of red tape for 'em and got 'em machinery to make magnesium.

Just had lunch with Secretary Forrestal and three nice admirals and an asst. sec. Had lots to eat too. They were trying to get me on their side on the reconversion plan. Kiss your mamma for me, tell grandmother and all the family hello.

Lots of love   Dad

*When I inquired about the mounting drive for Dad to
become Vice-President, he wrote me (and others) at the time,
sincerely stating that he did not want the job.*

WASHINGTON, D.C. TO DENVER, COLO.

Sunday A.M.
July 9, 1944

My dear Sweet Child:—

It was a very nice letter and I was so happy to get it in
the mail yesterday. Yes they are plotting against your dad.
Every columnist and prognosticator is trying to make
him V.P. against his will. It is funny how some people would
give a fortune to be as close as I am to it and I don't want it.

Bill Boyle, Max Rosenthal, Mr. Biffle and a dozen others
were on my trail yesterday with only that in view. Hope I
can dodge it. 1600 Pennsylvania is a nice address but I'd
rather not move in through the back door—or any other
door at sixty.

Got my two new summer suits yesterday. They look
very nice—a light grey one and a cream-colored one. Got
some gas tickets to take the car home. So you and your ma
can get around.

Jimmy Cromwell just called me and wanted to come
over for cocktails this P.M. I hope to be in Union town about
that time.

Glad you are having such a nice time. Have me a letter
at home. Kiss mamma.

Lots of love   Dad
XXXXXXX   OOO

Dad wrote me this letter about the Republican
nominee —which forecast the direction of the campaign.

WASHINGTON, D.C. TO INDEPENDENCE, MO.

Washington, D.C.
August 8, 1944

My dear Daughter:—

Your good letter came day before yesterday and was it
appreciated. Glad the church supper was good—hope
Kelsey's was too. Too bad you disappointed Mrs. Gage.
Maybe she'll recover—I don't care. Don't worry about that
St. Louis Republican meeting. I was going into the Union
Station to take the B + O as Dewey came out. There were
not ten people there to meet him. More people came and
spoke to your dad accidentally than came to meet Mr. Dewey
on purpose. That can't be so good and I just now happened
to think of its significance.

You should have seen your pa fall in the river. Just
stood up and sat down in the water—clear over my head
without getting my shoes wet. The feet stayed in the boat.
I'm not sure I wasn't purposely ducked. Anyway they had
something to laugh and talk about. Sam Rayburn really
enjoyed it. Said that I'm now a full-fledged member of Jack
Cochran's Club.

This is going to be a tough, dirty campaign and you've
got to help your dad protect your good mamma. Nothing
can be said of me that isn't old and unproven—so this little
district attorney will try to hit me by being nasty to my
family. You must remember that I never wanted or went
after the nomination—but now we have it, (to save the
Democratic Party—so the Southerners and A.F. of L. and
R.R. Labor say) we must win and make 'em like it. Maybe
your dad can make a job of the fifth wheel office.

But you must help me keep all the family in line. Most
of 'em on both sides are prima donnas and we must keep
our eyes on the ball. Lots + lots of love   Dad

On August 18, 1944, Dad met President Roosevelt at the
White House. Later that same day, he wrote me a letter about it.

WASHINGTON, D.C. TO INDEPENDENCE, MO.

Washington, D.C.
August 18, 1944

My dear Margie:— Today may be one in history. Your dad
had a most informal luncheon with Mr. Roosevelt on the
terrace behind the White House, under a tree set out by old
Andy Jackson. Mrs. Boettinger was also present. She
expected your mother to come with me. When I went to
leave, the Pres. gave me a rose out of the vase in the center
of the small round table at which we ate for your mother,
and Mrs. B. gave me one for you. You should have seen your
pa walking down Connecticut Ave. to the Mayflower
Hotel, where a date with Mr. Hannegan was in prospect,
with his hat blown up by the wind (so he looked like a
college boy—grey hair and all). And two rose buds in his
hand. He should have been arrested as a screwball but
wasn't.

I told the President, how very grateful I was for his
putting the finger on me for V.P. and how I appreciated the
honor etc. etc. ad lib. and then we discussed sealing wax
and many things to make the country run—for the
Democrats.

You should have been with me at the press conference
in the front room of the White House Offices. Hope I made
no hits, no runs, no errors—particularly no errors.

We had roast sardines (think they were Maine baby
halibut) on toast, peas, beans, tomatoes, asparagus all
mixed up in a salad—very nice when you left out the peas +
carrots, and lots of good brown toast, then pickled
clingstone peaches and a teaspoon full of coffee all served
on beautiful White House china and with lovely silver and
butlers etc. galore.

When we first sat down there were movie-cameras set up all around. We were in our shirt sleeves. The Pres. took his coat off and I had to. Told him if I'd known that was what he intended to do I'd have put on a clean shirt and he said he had that very morning. Well so had I. Then the flashlight newspaper picture boys had an inning equal almost to the box at Chicago. The President got tired or hungry and said "now boys one more that's enough" and it ended.

You'll see it all in the movies and in the papers. Hope to see you on Monday. Keep up those music lessons and I'm anxious to know what the surprise is. Chopin's Opus 42? Rigandon? Pollaca Brilliante [sic]? What?

Kiss mamma. Here's some expenses.
Lots + lots of love.
                                    Dad

With my grandmother Wallace and a friend of hers.

Just a nice chatty note about what was going on.

CHICAGO, ILL. TO INDEPENDENCE, MO.

Sept. 18, '44

Dear Margie:— I ran across this one yesterday in the
Chicago Sun. It struck me as something I'd seen and heard
before—not in the exact words maybe but something like it.
So—take warning and sleep more. If your dad had done that
perhaps he wouldn't have the "heaves" now.

You should have seen your mother getting off the train
in front of about a half dozen photographers. She stood up
exceptionally well. We had the Bowmans[?] up for lunch in
this swanky apartment. I have two, you know, a very gaudy
one at the Morrison too where I see the drunken
Legionnaires and contribute somewhat to making them
that way.

We went out to see Helen and Eugene yesterday
afternoon and then went to the Ill. Governor's party at the
Palmer House and the Ill. State Commanders Party at the
Sherman. Both grand affairs—more gold braid and spit and
polish than you could shake a stick at.

We have the nice detective sergeant and his pal as our
escort. They take us everywhere and don't let us out of their
sight.

I'm going to speak at 11:00 A.M. and your ma and Helen
are going to listen—maybe.

Hope you had a grand time at Columbia but wish you'd
have come with us.

Lots of love

Dad

I had been rather shocked by the way some of the local politicians had handled, or rather failed to handle, their liquor at the election celebration. I wrote to Dad about this and this was his reply.

BRADENTON, FLA. TO WASHINGTON, D.C.

Bradenton, Florida
December 3, 1944

My dear Daughter:— If you knew how much pleasure your good letter gave your dad when he arrived here you'd have one waiting on every occasion where he arrives at a new destination.

Your views on Mr. Boyle and the other middle-aged soaks are exactly correct. I like people who can control their appetites and their mental balance. When that isn't done I hope you'll always scratch them off your list. It is a shame about Boyle. I picked him up off the street in Kansas City, because I thought he'd been mistreated by the people out there for whom he'd worked. He had the chance of a lifetime to become a real leader in politics and to have made a great name for himself. John Barleycorn got the best of him and so far as I'm concerned I can't trust him again. You see what it means to a man's family when he does things that way. Mrs. Boyle and those two lovely children will be the real ones to suffer, not the fat Mr. Boyle.

Well it looks as if I may get three days' rest, really and truly. It is a little cool down here as a result of Saturday's cold wave which followed me in from Kansas City, but I had a good sun, both this morning and the colonel and I are going out on the Gulf tomorrow where we'll get plenty of sunshine.

It was impossible for me to dodge the publicity.
Reporters were at the train at Memphis, Birmingham,
Jacksonville, Tampa and one was in the front yard when we
arrived at the colonel's home. He took care of me in good
order!

The party and wedding must have been very grand.
I'm glad your school is becoming more interesting. Yes
I'd like to go to the Opera on Dec. 13. I'll be home Sunday
Dec. 10th at 1:00 P.M. on the Seaboard Air Line. Hope you and
your mother can meet me.

Wish you and mother were here. It is a lovely place.
There are four bedrooms and three bathrooms, three acres
of yard space + the bay in front. He has some beautiful
paintings. Kiss mamma, lots of love   Dad
    XXXXX   OOOO   XXX

Harry Truman to Margaret Truman

Presidential Years (1946– 51)

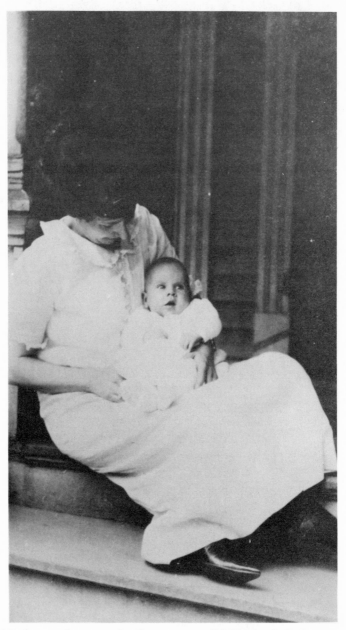

Mother and me on the front steps of 219 North Delaware, Independence, Missouri.

The piano had fallen through the ceiling in the White House!

WASHINGTON, D.C. TO INDEPENDENCE, MO.

June 12, 1946

Dear Margie:— Your note came yesterday afternoon. I don't know why the delay. I imagine that you and Aunt Beuf did have some trouble keeping warm if Aunt Nat thought she was hot. Ninety five is pretty warm and I know from experience how you and Aunt May hate fresh air. Both of you are sort of French I think in that. The French never raise a window because night air is bad for the health! So they say.

Your pop has missed you and your mama very much. They are fixing the hole in the middle of the hallway, opposite my study door. All the rugs are rolled back and a great scaffold has been constructed under the hole. Looks like they intend to hang a murderer in the White House Hallway. There are some gentlemen in the Congress—and out of it, who would take great pleasure in hanging your dad on that scaffold! But they'll have to catch him first. I hope to dry some of their political hides on a frame before I'm through. I'm giving 'em both barrels of the blunderbuss from here out.

When you need funds let me know. Your Aunt Mary is going home today. I tried to get her a plane reservation but couldn't. Jack Frye is taking her in his plane. You should go and see her and your country grandmother as soon as you can and you should call up your cousin Harry and congratulate him. I don't know what the Trumans and the Wallaces and the Campbells and the Gates and the others of the clans will do for a clearing house when your dad's gone.

I don't suppose you'd take over? It's a lot of fun making prima donnas happy—male + female. Maybe you want to be one! Look at the Supreme Court—and my Cabinet.

XXXXXXX Lots of love   Dad
OOOOOOO

*Mother and I went back to Independence and Dad had gone to
the Watergate to hear a concert. (He wanted to hear the whole
thing but people discovered him there and he had to leave.) That
was also the summer I decided to read all of Shakespeare and Dad
complimented me on that.*

WASHINGTON, D.C. TO INDEPENDENCE, MO.

June 17, 1946

Dear Margie:— The records came this morning. I would not
have received your letter nor your mother's if I hadn't raised the
roof. They were holding them at the central post office here. I
told Mr. Hannegan how very efficient his outfit here in town
is—and then you and your ma throw bucks at my postmaster in
Independence.

The records came and I am playing them over + over. It is
a very pretty piece. The National Symphony played it for me and
gave me a score to read.

I drove down to the Watergate all alone in the big open car
and stayed until the intermission. Wish you and your mama had
been here to go with me.

I am getting to be quite a gadabout with both of you away.
I've been to see Olsen + Johnson, went to a lawn party at the
Joe Davies' for the Gridiron Club, went to church yesterday
morning, to John Sullivan's for a cocktail party, called on Bob
Hannegan and went to the Watergate.

I suppose some crackpot columnist will have something to
say about it. But I don't care what they say. I am sending you a
copy of the Watergate program (enclosed).

Hope you are having a nice time reading Shakespeare—you
see what education does for a good mind. It just shows you how
very little you know. I'm glad you are finding how necessary it is
to keep finding out things. You can never stop when you get
going. I always wanted to know about things firsthand—it helps
in this job.

Kiss your ma for me and tell your Aunts, Uncles and
Grandmas hello for me.

Lots of love
OOOOOOO   Dad
XXXXXX

Dad sent me a bill for $1.50 to tune the White House piano. I still have that bill.

WASHINGTON, D.C. TO INDEPENDENCE, MO.

June 29, 1946

Dear Margie:— I am enclosing a musical score of Mozart's <u>Eine kleine Nachtmusik</u> which was given to me for the Watergate concert. I had to leave before they got to it but they gave me the credit for listening. I have been playing the records too.

There is also enclosed a bill for $1.50 for tuning the White House piano in Andrew Johnson's time—1865. Thought you'd like to have it. There is also enclosed a letter from Sen. McKellar enclosing one asking you to go to Chattanooga for a cotton ball. Tell the Senator what you can or cannot do. It is a promotion scheme.

Your mamma will be here today—I wish you would too. We've put air conditioners in her rooms, have closed up the hole in the 3rd floor and things are shining and clean as a pin—except your room looks rather deserted and forlorn.

Hope you are having a nice time. Mayes + Fields and Julia and Wilma ask me about you at least twice a week.

Tell your grandmother hello and also your aunts + uncles. Go and see your country aunt and grandma when you can.

        Lots of love   Dad

XXXXXX
OOOOO

Dad was always confident that I could become a successful singer on my own, without "do[ing] a Roosevelt stunt" or using the White House to get ahead.

WASHINGTON, D.C. TO INDEPENDENCE, MO.

Dear Sistie:— I am lonesome this morning—thought maybe I might get a letter from my little girl. But I suppose she's busy with breathing exercises, vocal gymnastics and young gentlemen and so hasn't had the time.

Your dad was very much pleased at your progress. You know you could make a right good income if you wanted to do a Roosevelt stunt and sell your White House connection by selling records. But I'd much rather you'd make good on merit as a capable young lady with a good voice. Of course I'm inclined to be a little bit prejudiced in your favor but I think you are a capable young lady with a good voice, good looks and above all good manners. Now don't lose the good manners for a career. Very few prima donnas are worth having around and I don't want that to happen to Margie.

I've been signing bills, seeing customers and reading veto messages ever since I got here. Hope to finish up by Friday and then go riding on the Williamsburg for a week or so with no one around but the help. Maybe I can get some sleep.

I am walking to church this morning and I hope sleeping most of the rest of the day.

Tomorrow is Aunt Mary's birthday. Hope you didn't forget it.

Kiss mommy + lots of love to you

XXXXXXXXX   Dad
OOOOOOOOO

*Dad and I knew that my attempts to launch a musical career
would be used by political hatchetmen as excuses for sneak attacks
on the White House. In his letter, he worried about my career and
gave me some advice.*

BERMUDA TO INDEPENDENCE, MO.

Bermuda, August 23, 1946

My dear Daughter:—

Your letter was a nice one and highly appreciated by your
old dad. I am glad you are working hard at your music. If you
love it enough to give it all you have nothing can stop you. There
is only one thing I ask—please don't become a temperamental
case. It is hard to keep from it. I know—and no one knows
better than I. But it is not necessary nor does it help in your
public relations. It makes no friends and to succeed at anything
you must have friends on whom you can rely. That is just as
true of a musical career as it is of a political one or a business
career.

You now have the educational background, you have had
the contacts with people so that you should have no trouble in
that respect. Keep your moral background and always deal
honorably, but in contracts watch your proper interests
carefully and have a legal expert always to read the "fine print"
for you.

Now that's out of my mind I wish you and your mother
were here. This is a paradise you dream about but hardly ever
see. I don't think I'd want it as a steady diet but for my purpose it
is ideal. This island is a coral one 22 miles long in the shape of a
fish hook. Look at the map in the encyclopedia. All the houses
are built of coral with coral roofs as white as snow.

They saw the coral out with a handsaw and it hardens and
then they paint it with concrete and whitewash it or paint it.
The houses are pink, white, red, tan and most other colors.

The sea is blue as the sky and it is 84°. I take a walk on shore every morning and then have breakfast, take a sunbath on deck and a swim alongside the ship, have lunch, a nap and this afternoon I'm going deep-sea fishing! Beat that if you can. Called on the Governor General yesterday. He met me at the dock in an open carriage with a coachman + footman up, drawn by two spanking grey horses. We rode through Hamilton in truly royal state, to Government House on top of a hill overlooking the town. Then we rode back to the boat in the same style and back to the yacht. It was a pleasant experience. There are 33,000 people on the islands, ten thousand white and the rest colored. It is funny as can be to hear these blacks talk with an Oxford accent.

Well, I went fishing southwest of the Islands about five miles over a coral reef. Caught three very beautiful fish weighing from four to about ten pounds. One of them, the smallest, was red, one was tan with white spots and the other was a bright yellow with white stripes on him. You never saw anything prettier but they don't stay that way. After they are out a while they turn dark fast but they say they are good to eat. We'll try my catch tomorrow. Ted caught a big brown fish and Capt. Foskett caught four not so large as mine. The rest caught none. Clifford almost fell overboard, Vaughan got seasick and Allen told me how good he is with fish but they didn't take to him.

Here's a piece about you from the Sunday Post-Dispatch, also some expense money. Kiss mommy for me. Tell all the rest hello.

      Lots of love   Dad.
      XXXXXX   OOOOOOO

Although he treated the subject lightly, Dad sometimes liked
to think that the White House was haunted.

WASHINGTON, D.C. TO INDEPENDENCE, MO.

September 9, 1946

Dear Margie:— It was good to get your good letter and hope
the voice is continuing to improve and I'm sure it is. Your
mother said you had made some new records with the flute
which she said were lovely. I'd like to hear them, but
according to the latest information it will be some time
before I do.

The commandant at West Point has invited us all up
then for the Oklahoma game Sept. 28th. But I guess I'll have
to tell him you and your ma won't be along. She said you
weren't expecting to come back until the middle of October.

I told your mother a "haunt" story which you'd better
have her read to you. This old place cracks and pops all
night long and you can very well imagine that Old Jackson
or Andy Johnson or some other ghost is walking. Why
they'd want to come back here I could never understand. It
is a very nice prison but a prison nevertheless. No man in
his right mind would want to come here of his own accord.
There are a lot of them who are not in their right minds
I'd say.

Your Uncle Vivian called me from the Statler last night
and is coming over for breakfast. I don't know why he didn't
come here in the first place. Even if the old wreck is torn up
from the cellar to garret I could have put him up.

The weather is hot as summertime. I hope yours has
cleared up. You say you are well-heeled so I won't ship you
any money this time. What did you think of that pretty piece
of plaid? Harry Vaughan bought a red one for his daughter
and I had him get me the blue one for you. How did your ma
like her pocketbook?

Well write to me when you have time. This is a lonesome place.

Lots of love.

                    Dad

XXXXXXXXX

OOOOOO

Sorry Doc Graham's medicine didn't work.

Uncle George Wallace with me
at about eighteen months.

In this letter, he discussed possible stage names for me (while admitting to his preference for my using my real name) and joked about the supposed ghosts in the White House.

WASHINGTON, D.C. TO INDEPENDENCE, MO.

September 13, 1946

Dear Daughter:— Glad you were pleased with your sweaters and plaid goods. The sweaters are very fine cashmere and specially woven. The plaid is real Scotch and came from Scotland.

Of course I'll miss you, but if you are going to train your voice the way to train it is to work at it. So I'll look for you in October. There has been so much said about assumed names etc. that I don't think you'll get by with the one talked about although it is a nice name. Now there are a lot of good names in the family on both sides. For instance, Mary Jane Holmes, your great-grandmother, Harriet Louisa Gregg, another great-grandmother, Matilda Middleton, a great-grandmother. Margaret Gates is alliterative. And Mary Margaret Gates would look good in headlines and Peggy Gates would probably catch 'em.

I also have some partiality for Mary Margaret Truman. Mr. Dooley in his column some years ago said safecrackers and stage stars were the only great professions which recognized assumed names. He may have had something there.

Now about those ghosts. I'm sure they're here and I'm not half so alarmed at meeting up with any of them as I am at having to meet the live nuts I have to see every day. I'm sure old Andy could give me some good advice and probably teach me some good swear words to use on Molotov and DeGaul [sic]. And I am sure Old Grover Cleveland could tell me some choice remarks to make to some political leaders, and Hebrew Rabbis I know. So I won't lock my doors or bar them either if any of the old coots in the pictures out in the hall want to come out of their frames for a friendly chat.

Work hard, be a nice young lady and do what you do with all the energy you have and you'll come out on top. Sometimes hard work will get you too far on top—look at your pop.

Lots of love
                    Dad   OOO
XXXXXXXXX

My outfit was the latest in
children's wear about 1926.

*Dad worried about picking out a successful stage name for
me, and that served as a springboard for a short lecture on
the qualities that make for a successful President.*

WASHINGTON, D.C. TO INDEPENDENCE, MO.

September 17, 1946

My dear Sistie:—

Here is a telegram from a nut over in Connecticut who
admits it! The only reason I'm sending it to you is because it
[is] signed by a very euphonious name—Matilda Jelal. What
a stage name that would make—and you might see visions
too! And you have to see visions to get real headlines. Look
at Henry Wallace, Pepper, Huey Long, Bilbo, Talmadge of
Georgia—and remember Joe Stalin, Hitler, Mussolini,
Franco, Perfivio Diaz and a dozen others.

But you are not interested in them you are thinking of
Adelina Patti, Alice Nielsen, Melba Tetrazini, Margarita
Silva, Sembrach[?] and a dozen others of the great opera.
Well I'm hoping—if you want to, that you can join them and
put all of them in second place.

But don't be too much disappointed if you only equal
them. Your pop always knew what he would do when he
became the President—and look how it turned out! To be a
good President I fear a man can't be his own mentor. He
can't live the Sermon on the Mount. He must be a
Micheaveli [sic], Louis XI of France, Cesar Borgia,
Napoleon's chief minister (Talleyrand), whose name
has escaped me, a liar, double-crosser and an unctious
religio (Richelieu), a hero and a whatnot to be successful.
So I probably won't be, thanks be to God. But I'm having
a lot of fun trying the opposite approach. Maybe it
will win.

When oh when will you be back here? I told your mother to wear a red carnation in her hat so I'd know her when she got off the train and that I'd wear a blue suit, grey hat and black shoes. I'll never know you I'm sure when you get back here. So you'd better wear your plaid skirt and pink sweater—and let your hair be its "natural" color.

Wish you and your ma were here for next Sunday. Miss Snyder will pay me a visit on my boat as Queen of the President's Regatta. I'm sure it will be nice.

Kiss your mammy, tell your two grandmas hello and also your various aunts + uncles. Here's some financial help.   XXXXX

Lots of love   Dad   OOO
OOOO   XXXXXXXX

As busy as Dad was, he wanted to be consulted by me before I signed any singing contracts.

WASHINGTON, D.C. TO INDEPENDENCE, MO.

September 25, 1946

Dear Margie:— The record was fine. This old machine we have, however, is no good. Will have to have it worked on I guess. Your voice shows you've been working hard. It seems to have both volume and a beautiful tone.

Don't let any of the smart boys get you into a contract until you've consulted your pa on the details. I'm glad you decided to stay at home and study rather than go to the wilds of that terrible town at the mouth of the Hudson.

Keep working and I am sure if you want to badly enough you can make the grade. It takes lots and lots of hard work and concentration. Your dad knows what that means. It seems awful long since I've seen you. Maybe you'd better send me your picture.

Lots of love
                    Dad

We made ma phone anyway.

I stayed in Missouri to continue my studies, but Dad was trying to lure me back to the White House, as you can see in his description of his visit to West Point for an Army football game.

WASHINGTON, D.C. TO INDEPENDENCE, MO.

October 1, 1946

My dear Margie:—

   Your mama and I were very glad to get "belated" letter. I hope you won't be too busy to send us another one. We are always glad to get them. You write interestingly and perhaps when you arrive at Schuman-Heink's age and your good voice cracks you can become a great storywriter.
   You should have been here to go to West Point with me. Twenty-one hundred bosoms were all aflutter when I arrived hoping to see my daughter. So just to get even I had to stand them up and make 'em quake in the knees for me! They put on a beautiful parade and review and the game was interesting if full of errors.
   I saw some interesting things in the military museum and had a pleasant day all around winding up with the usual reception and handshakes at the commandant's house. Gen. Danford was there as was his Mrs. Bill Mox was there visiting a cadet. So were Jed + Mrs. Johnson of Okla. So—you see what you missed besides all those fluttering hearts.
   I hope your concert program is progressing. The Home Sweet Home record was lovely. Madam Patti will have to look to her laurels. Why don't you send me all those records? I can make this old machine play 'em after a fashion and I can set up your picture and make believe you're there anyway.
   By the way I wish you'd send me a late news photo so I won't forget how you look. Now keep working and write often. I suppose ma is writing you too.

Lots of love   Mama's phone at Mrs. Lester's is
        Dad   Chestnut 6322. Aunt Mary sent it.
XXXXX   OO
OOO

*Dad was still trying to lure me to the White House, now with
some joking comments about how long it had been since he
had seen me.*

WASHINGTON, D.C. TO INDEPENDENCE, MO.

October 12, 1946

Dear Margie:— Was glad to read your letter, which your ma
was kind enough to let me see. I think you'd better send me
a picture—a late one so I'll be sure and recognize you when
I come home. I am afraid the four or five pictures I have on
my desks will not be a good likeness now—particularly one
[of you] on a tricycle in coat and panties.

If you are really turning into the prima donna you
want to be you may by this time weigh some two hundred
ten and be as buxom as Melba or Lillian Russell by all the
rules. I want to be sure.

This place without you is very very dreary. I don't
know what your mamma and I will do when you go on tour.
I guess I'll have to go to an orphan's home and get me a
substitute. How would that do? It might work.

Your Uncle Vivian and your Cousin Ralph are here.
They stayed at the White House last night and I think
enjoyed themselves.

When are you sending me some more records? This
old machine isn't worth a damn and I can fill in with
imagination what I know the songs are like.

Here is some expense money.

Lots of love
Dad

XXXX
OOOOO

Some nut destroyed a picture of Dad that was in the National Gallery.

WASHINGTON, D.C. TO INDEPENDENCE, MO.

October 19, 1946

Dear Margie:— I am enclosing a picture of your ma taken on the front porch of the W.H. She seems to be completely disgusted with the procedure. I wish she'd have smiled a little bit.

Hope your music is coming along all right. It looks now as if we'll leave here Thursday Oct. 31 for home and get there Friday and leave there Nov. 5 at 9:30 A.M. and get here the 6th. So you won't get a ride in the Cow after all. I hope we have no train wrecks.

Somebody went to the National Gallery and cut a hole in my picture last night. It is one the young Virginia painter made and a very good one. He evidently thought well of it because he was insuring it for $10,000. Somebody had gotten left out on meat or a job or something like that. It is funny how human beings react. They always want more from their leaders than they can give them and they always like to put mud on their Presidents. That's bad for the Presidents!

Tell grandma hello and call your country one. Remember me to all your Aunts + Uncles + Cousins.

Lots of love
                Dad

Dad made a speech to the UN, which went over better than he had expected.

WASHINGTON, D.C. TO INDEPENDENCE, MO.

October 26, 1946

Dear Margie:— It was nice to talk with you last night. I hope you'll wear a red carnation in your hair when you come to the train on Friday so I'll be sure to recognize you! It's been a very long time you know since I've seen my baby.

We had a nice trip to New York. Managed to get your mother aboard the Cow at 2:30 and we were at La Guardia field at 3:40. They had policemen every ten feet and plainclothesmen everywhere. Evidently they'd had some threats. They objected to my riding in an open car although the streets were lined with people who wanted to see the curiosity who is President of the United States.

The speech seemed to go over well. Even the Ruskies came up and very cordially congratulated me. It is very hard to make a speech when half the audience can't understand what is said. There was just a circle of deadpans in the front rows.

We went to the Waldorf where we were met in the apartment by the Stewarts. Your ma put on her best bib and tucker and we went down to the ball room for a reception. Shook hands with 835 people in one hour flat and then went to the train. Jim and Mrs. Byrnes came back with us and Mr. Byrnes ran like a phonograph for 3 hours and thirty minutes. No one else had to say a word. We went to the show at G.W. night before last. Drucie was the main character in the show and she did excellently. They all did. The Snyders and the Lingos[?] sat by us. The show was as good as professionals. Won't it be grand if you turn out to be the singer of the age and Drucie the actress? Your ma is sending program. Here's a little dough.

    Lots of love
           Dad

See you Friday I hope.

Although he was in the midst of his struggles with John L.
Lewis, he found time to take my career seriously. In the
second part of this letter, he was still angry when he realized
how the Navy brass had upstaged him at the launching of the
Missouri *two years earlier.*

WASHINGTON, D.C. TO NEW YORK CITY

Thursday, November 14, 1946

My dear Margie:— I have read your letter to your mother +
me and one from Mrs. Strickler about your interview with
Mr. Jagel. I am happy that he thinks you have a good
chance to sing successfully. Of course, if that is what you
want—that is what I want you to have. It seems to me you
have gone about your career in the right way.

You have finished your college. You have worked
long and hard to get your voice in condition for the final
trials. You are willing to take the necessary advice from
honest people on what to do to make your preliminary
trials. Your daddy will support you to the end on whatever
it takes to make these trials. But daughter, don't fool
yourself. You know what it takes.

Your dad doesn't want you to fail publicly. Not that he
wouldn't be for you win, lose or draw, but because of
conditions a failure would be unbearable for you. You
won't fail! You have your dad's tenacity and your ma's
contrariness, and together they should make you.

Now you'd better tell me what the expenses are to date.
We must not be charity patients of anybody.

I am going to fly to Florida on Sunday, because Doc
thinks I need some <u>Sunshine</u>. It will probably rain all the
time we are there.

The damned navy here have tried to give me an
impossible schedule. As you know every Admiral within
nine hundred miles will want to be seen with the President.
But they are going to be disappointed. I'll never forget what
the same Admirals did to me and my sweet daughter at the
launching of the <u>Missouri</u>.

The same admirals should read Josh Billings—should have read him before the launching. He said "Always be nice to your pore [sic] relations—they may suddenly become rich someday and it will be hard to explain."

Would you like to fly to Missouri with your dad on Sunday Nov. 24 to celebrate your grandmother's birthday? If I can get your mamma to go we'd stay for dinner and come right back.

Here is a little money. If you need more, say so.

Lots of love from your <u>lonesome</u> dad.
XXXXXXXXX
OOOOOO

Mother, Dad and me. Why did I turn my back?

Dad wrote this letter from the airplane, The Sacred Cow.

ABOARD THE SACRED COW TO NEW YORK CITY

Somewhere in the air in Kentucky
November 24, 1946

My dear Daughter:— I am sorry you couldn't come home
and take this trip with me. Your mother wouldn't. I guess
it's a good thing she didn't, for I've never had a rougher trip
over Missouri. Result of the election, I guess,—and a 70 mile
headwind. Your ma'd have been scared stiff. But if
conditions had allowed I sure wish you'd both been there.

Mary had outdone herself in cooking a turkey and
all the trimmings—backed up with ice cream and a
beautiful birthday cake for your ninety-four-year-old
grandmother. Your Aunt Luella and Mary were waiters
to all your Uncle Vivian's family including the
great-grandchildren—you were the only absentee
grandchild. Mamma's first question was, "Where is
Margaret?"

We left from Andrews Field at 7:50 and fooled the
goons. It took 5 hrs. 10 mins. We'll go back in three and a
half with some tail wind. Have just witnessed a most
beautiful sunset from 9,400 ft. Is your arm paralyzed?
Here's some more dough. Don't you be a charity patient.
Vibration?

OOOO   Lots of love   Dad   OOO

*This letter contains a sprinkling of his philosophical
thoughts.*

WASHINGTON, D.C. TO INDEPENDENCE, MO.

Sunday, December 21, 1946

Dear Margie:—

You don't know how much your old daddy appreciated
your good letter. Glad you had the chance to sleep in a lower
for once. Did Vietta sleep in the upper? I've been wondering
where she slept. You must have had a grand trip from St.
Louis with the snooty and talkative Mrs. Sonter. When we
were kids she and her sister and George never felt that your
pop was good enough to associate with the children of a
college president—even if the college was in a fading
condition. But I never cared. She had a black sheep brother
named Paul who was a regular guy and who always had a
good time with us roughnecks of the lower strata. Your ma
was upper crust too but she wasn't snooty like the Bryants.
You understand you don't know anything about this.
Because since those days your pa never pretends he
remembers and he's done favors and was glad to for all
of them including the lowbrow black sheep.

Now I heard you say the other evening when we were
discussing your career that you were after the big money.
Now that I don't approve of. I want you to have artistic
perfection—and the money will come of itself. I want you to
be a truly great singer and not Kate Smith or a radio
crooner. When you have attained artistic perfection all the
rest will come. Service then to the pleasure of people will
make you great. And I mean service to the higher instincts
of the people. There are lowbrows who'll never appreciate
the good you do who make burlesque singers a success. I
don't want you to be burlesque—I want you to be the real
thing and I am sure, now, that you can.

So take it in stride and do it right. It is the hard way but the best way. When your pa ran for the Eastern Judge the wise old boys told me you can never do any good in that office. I did though because I gave service to the people. I didn't want to be Presiding Judge. I had to take it. I didn't want to be Senator—it was forced upon me and you know the rest. I worked at each job to put the best in me into it for service—and look at my most terrible windup. Maybe I shouldn't have mentioned it.

Kiss mamy for me + tell your grandmas your aunts, uncles and cousins hello.

XXXXXXXXX   Dad
OOOO

Aunt Natalie and me in the back yard.

Dad often missed important holidays because, as he made clear in this letter, work always came first.

WASHINGTON, D.C. TO INDEPENDENCE, MO.

Sunday Dec. 22, '46

Dear Margie:—

I'm sitting at your mother's desk surrounded by at least 5,000 Christmas cards and packages of loot intended for her and you. You'll have a great time opening them when you get back—when you do.

It was nice to talk to you just now and I am as disappointed as you are that I won't be home Christmas Eve. But I have a job to do and it comes first. I didn't ask for it and didn't want it. But now I have it, all I have (not enough) must go into it. Your pop, for some unknown reason, can't be a skirt even at the risk of making you and your mother unhappy.

I'm glad you decided to eat Mitchell's ice cream, good or not. That shows a fundamental right spirit—and you should and do, now understand why, if it can be arranged, some government employees should have Christmas Eve with their babies. One of the babies is only two months old. "Conscientious" objectors are picketing at the White House today. That's why I'm in your ma's office. Hitler would have had us if they had their way. Very few are "conscientious." Here is the card (enclosures). Kiss mommy. Lots of love   Dad

XXXXXXXXXXXXXXX

Dad was right when he said he had given me "a good name and good advice."

WASHINGTON, D.C. TO NEW YORK CITY

February 6, 1947

Dear Margie:— Received your notice just now. I suppose you have heard by this time that our good old friend Max Gardner died of a heart attack this morning as he was preparing to sail for London. He is a great loss. Was a ten strike as Ambassador to Great Britain and will be difficult to replace.

Go ahead and get that nice case for me to give your mamma. I will tell your grandmother not to get gloves. I can't think of anything else to get her and she won't tell me anything to get.

I hope your work is getting results. It takes work, work and more work to get satisfactory results, as your pop can testify. Don't go off the deep end on contracts until you know for sure what you are getting—and what you have to offer.

I am only interested in your welfare and happy future and I stand ready to do anything to contribute to that end. But remember that good name and honor are worth more than all the gold and jewels ever mined. Remember what old man Shakespeare said "Who steals my purse steals trash, but who filches my good name takes that which enriches not himself and makes me poor indeed." A good name and good advice is all your dad can give you.

I am counting the days until you come home.

Lots + lots of love
Dad

This note was written when I was about to make my debut.

WASHINGTON, D.C. TO ?

Feb. 28, 1947

Dear Margie:—

    Here's a little dough in case you need R.R. tickets to some mysterious town.

    Now don't get scared, you can do it! And if anyone says you can't I'll bust him in the snoot.

    Lots of love
              Dad

My favorite tricycle.
I was four years old.

I hope this letter will be read by the historians who try to depict Dad as plunging recklessly and even enthusiastically into the Cold War.

KEY WEST, FLA. TO WASHINGTON, D.C.

> Key West, Florida.
> March 13, 1947

Dear Margie:— We had a very pleasant flight from Washington. Your old dad slept for 750 or 800 miles—three hours—and we were making from 250 to 300 miles an hour. No one not even me (your mother would say I) knew how very tired and worn to a frazzle the chief executive had become. This terrible decision I had to make had been over my head for about six weeks. Although I knew at Potsdam that there is no difference in totalitarian or police states, call them what you will, Nazi, Fascist, Communist or Argentine Republics. You know there never was but one idealistic example of communism. That is described in the Acts of the Apostles.

The attempt of Lenin, Trotsky, Stalin et al. to fool the world and the American crackpots' association, represented by Joe Davies, Henry Wallace, Claude Pepper and the actors and artists in immoral Greenwich Village, is just like Hitler's and Mussolini's so called socialist states.

Your pop had to tell the world just that in polite language.

Now in addition to that terrible—and it is terrible—decision, your good old 94-year-old grandmother of the 1860 generation was unlucky and broke her leg—you—the "apple of my eye"—my sweet baby always had bad luck with your first appearance. Well daughter the dice roll—sometimes they are for you—sometimes they are not.

But I earnestly believe they were for you this time. I am just as sure as I can be that Sunday night at 8:00 P.M. another great soprano will go on the air. So don't worry about anything—just go on and sing as you sang that "Home Sweet Home" record for your dad—and nothing can stop you—even the handicap of being the Daughter of President Truman!

Then you come back to the White House and let me arrange a nice warm rest for you and your lovely mamma and we'll go on from there.

You must learn self-discipline—that is you must eat what you should, drink what you should—and above all sleep <u>at night</u> and always give people the benefit of <u>good</u> intentions until they are <u>proven</u> bad. Don't put your comfort and welfare above those around you. In other words be a good commonsense Missouri woman—daughter of your mother—in my opinion the greatest woman on earth—I want you to be second.

More love than you can realize now.

Dad

In between worrying about the Russians and the 8oth Congress, he worried about my career and advised me not to let success go to my head.

WASHINGTON, D.C. TO NEW YORK CITY

May 14, 1947

Dear Margie:—

Tom Clark sent me this note. When you get to these towns I'm sure you'll find your reservations at these hotels, because they wouldn't want to put you up at a dump.

When you go to the hotel not mentioned by Tom see the manager yourself and explain to him that your personal maid must stay with you and you'll have no trouble I'm sure.

The best of luck, your dad's praying for you. Wish I could go along and smooth all the rough spots—but I can't and in a career you must learn to overcome the obstacles without blowing up. Always be nice to all the people who can't talk back to you. I can't stand a man or woman who bawls out underlings to satisfy an ego.

Again good luck + success.
Lots of hugs + kisses.

Dad

*A friend of Dad's gave me a small piece of oil well which Dad
thought I should hold on to. (I sold it a few years later.)*

WASHINGTON, D.C. TO INDEPENDENCE, MO.

Wed. July 16, 1947

Dear Margie:— I was most happy to get your good but very
late letter Sunday morning. It is very lonesome around here
even if I do work from daylight until dark. It is much nicer
when someone is around making a "noise." Then the
"ghosts" continue to walk up and down the hall and around
the study.

But my days are full up to the top. Had the Cabinet for
lunch Monday, and all the secretaries and ushers yesterday.
They seemed to have a good time and Pye helped Fields to
serve!

Mr. Helm's address is Caruthersville, Mo. He came in to
tell me goodbye yesterday, saying that his granddaughter
and Mrs. Helm had almost worn him out. The other
signature on the lease is Mr. Helm's. He also told me they'd
just brought in another 150 barrelswell! You'll [be] a rich
woman yet. Put that lease away and hang on to it. It will
bring you a $150 a month for the rest of your life. You
should write Mr. Helm and thank him for it.

I hope your lessons are working out to advantage. I
sure want that postponed concert tour to be a grand
success.

The canvas[?] are just beginning to bloom. They are only
18 inches high and do not obstruct the view as the tall ones
did. But the Jap beetles are eating the blooms. Had a wire
that your mamma had safely arrived in Denver.

Don't eat too much chocolate ice cream, be nice to your
aunts and go see your country grandma once in a while. Say
hello to Frank + George + your Aunts. Lots of love   Dad
XXXXXXXXXXXXXX

In spite of his tantalizing offer, I never did receive the ring.

WASHINGTON, D.C. TO INDEPENDENCE, MO.

July 19, 1947

Dear Daughter:— It was nice to talk to you last night. It
really kept the "ghosts" away. I didn't hear a single one last
night and I left all the doors open too because it is so hot. I
was up at 4:00 A.M. so as to get a letter to you, your ma and
your Aunt Mary.

I certainly would have been pleased to see that riot at
the station when you put your mother and grandmother on
the train. It must have been good.

I am enclosing your $2,000 Chinese which Mr. Beck of
Collier's gave me for you. It is worth about 15 cents in our
money. I think he told me he purchased $1,500,000 for
$200 and the next day he could have gotten it for $150.
Your bill is perhaps worth a nickel now. Anyway it's a nice
souvenir.

I am up at 5:00 A.M. to get this off to you because as I
told you last night I'm going down the river—(in a boat)
today and won't get home until Sunday night.

I've had a really strenuous week and the next one will
be just as bad. But we have to face the situation as it is. So it
will probably be August 2 before I get home. I'll know all
about Brazil by that time though and can give you some idea
of the time it will take. You might be able to do it. I hope so.

Do you need anything—money marbles or chalk, you
may have anything I have. You should see the most
beautiful and ancient ring the latest Arab visitor gave me. It
is a peculiar stone carved evidently in Ancient Egypt and
the ring itself was made before Christ. I can't get it on.
Maybe you can. Mrs. Ganey said they kept a special guard
with a drawn scimitar by it all the time night and day, so it
must be very valuable I guess. I'll get ranked out of it by a
certain young lady.

Tell your aunts and uncles hello and thanks, for me, for keeping you.

Lots of love
                        Dad
XXXXX
OOOOO

My Uncle Frank, who taught me how to drive a car, and me, age sixteen.

*Mamma Truman died on July 26th, and Dad was feeling
the loss when he wrote this letter on August 1st.*

WASHINGTON, D.C. TO INDEPENDENCE, MO.

August 1, 1947

Dear Margie:— Your nice letter was here when I returned. I
can't understand why you dislike to write letters when you
do them so well. Anyway your pop likes to get one—even if
they are spaced at long intervals.

Someday you'll be an orphan just as you dad is now. I
hope your work on the programs are successful.

Sam Rayburn was in to see me before he left for Texas
and told me that he had a very good friend in Dallas — a
grand dame apparently who is head of all the Democratic
women and who has as much money as the National City
Bank.

He said if you accepted any invitations he hoped you
would go to a tea at her house when you were in Dallas. I've
lost her name but will try to find it. Sam's my best friend in
the House—so if you can accommodate him all right.

I am going up to S_____ [?] today and will meet your
ma at Silver Springs on Monday as I return to town.

Wish you were coming back with her. This place is a
tomb without you + your mother.

I have been looking over the thousands of letters, cards
+ telegrams about your old grandmother. They come from
every state and every country and are very kind. Have heard
from the Pope, King George, King Mahai, Chiang Kai-Shek,
Dr. Kung[?], the Queen of Holland and every president in
the Western Hemisphere.

But the ones I appreciate most come from home. Heard
from men + women your mother + I went to school with—
some I hadn't heard from in 40 years.

Got one from the colored man who always waits on me at the Kansas City Club and one signed Fields, Pye and Prettyman, and one signed by all the Sergeants who guard my plane. I like them more than all the top-notchers. Your dad just can't appreciate formal stuffed shirt approach. Had letters, cards + wires from all Senators, House members + Governors, even Dewey + Taft.

    Lots of love.   Don't work too hard.

Dad

XXXXXXX
OOOOO

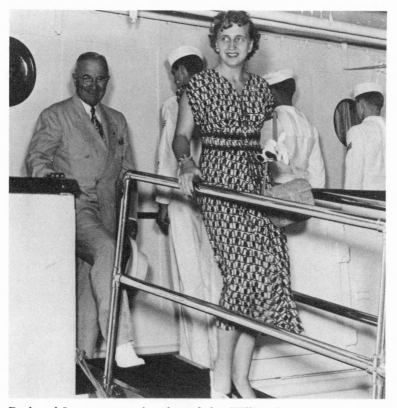

Dad and I are on a cruise aboard the *Williamsburg*.

*Dad discussed his difficulties in getting Congress to accept
his ideas, along with the importance of the proper handling
of the press, not only in his career but also in mine.*

WASHINGTON, D.C. TO INDEPENDENCE, MO.

October 1, 1947

My dear Daughter:— You notice I didn't address you as my
"baby" or my "pet." If you could understand how very much
I appreciate and how much of a lift your old and pestered
dad gets out of the communications I get from you—you
would at least send one-a-week.

Your letter of last Friday was, of course, most highly
appreciated. I'm glad you + your ma are not bothered with
salutes and I am most happy that champaigns [sic] are out.
Even if Mrs. Bidault likes it for France. I think it is an
invention of the devil and the vinegar trade. Barsac and
another white wine are much better and more in line with
good health.

I was sorry I didn't get to talk with you last Thursday,
but I was happy you answered the call on Sunday—but you
seemed anxious to terminate the conversation. I didn't
think you really felt that way but you gave that impression.
It makes no difference what impression you give him, he's
always for you win, lose or draw.

I've had the most terrible and terrific ten days since
April 12, 1945. I've worked from sunup to sundown and a
couple of hours before and after every day since the Monday
we returned from Brazil. Every Republican is trying to put
your pa in the hole and every Wallacite is making a
contribution in that direction—as is old Uncle Bill
Southern, Roy Roberts, Frank Kent, Bertie McCormick, and
his kinfolk Cissy Paterson. You know Bertie and his cousins
run the Chicago Tribune, New York Daily News +
the Times-Herald—all of them sabotage sheets. Their
owners and editors should have been shot for traitors in

1943. In Germany, in Japan and in Russia they would have been shot or put in forced labor camps. <u>They are still traitors</u>.

Now you are to start on a career and I want that career to be a grand success. I am sure it will be. But you must have <u>good</u> public relations and that means a good press and radio. I fear very much that you are not getting it. Use good judgment and try to get it. Your dad knows how to get it from experience. If you want advice ask him. <u>You can't win</u> without it no matter how good or how rich you may be. John D. Rockefeller found that out as has every successful singer and politician. I'm only telling you.

I want you to win on merit and I am sure you <u>can</u> win on merit—but if you do not have the proper presentation of that merit no one will know of it. Hard work and a pleasant disposition will win. Remember, photographers are working people who sell pictures. Help them sell them. Reporters are people who sell stories—help them sell stories.

The new American Legion Commander came in to see me today. He wants me to speak + you to sing at the Tomb of the Unknown Soldier on Nov. 11. I think we'd better. What shall I tell him. Kiss mamma + remember Aunt Mary has no one now. Lots + lots of love.

XXXXXXXXXXXX   Dad
OOOOOOOOO

Dad had to keep making speeches even with a sore throat.

WASHINGTON, D.C. TO INDEPENDENCE, MO.

October 10, 1947

Dear Margie:— I've been trying to get a letter off to you since your last one came—but no luck.

I had to make a radio speech to the country Sunday on food and it took all day Friday, Saturday and Sunday to get ready. Two Cabinet members and the Food Committee Chairman to co-ordinate and then my own to get ready. At 5:00 P.M. Sunday I had to put my foot down and say "Here's the way it will be." It came out all right and I believe is working.

Tuesday I went out to the 1st Baptist Church and listened to a dozen speeches and made a two minute talk myself.

Wednesday I had to speak at 1:30 P.M. to the women of the country. All the time I've had a hacking cough and had to take heroic measures to stop it so the public wouldn't hear me cough.

The cough is about well now. I've been going to bed at eight and getting up at seven and Doc had been spraying my nose and throat. So it ought to be well by now.

Hope your plans are going along in good shape. John Snyder told me that he + Drucie and maybe Mrs. S. were going. Your ma is too I think, but I'm afraid I'd upset the apple cart if I went to Pittsburgh. The Mayor and Senator Myers came in and asked me to come.

Have had a dizzy three weeks but hope to catch up by another one. Hope you have had that Blue Springs trip. How's Uncle Frank? Say hello to M [?] + George + Grandmother

Lots of love   Dad
OOOOOOO   XXXXX

I was on my first concert tour, and Dad and Mother were feeling lonely.

WASHINGTON, D.C. TO INDEPENDENCE, MO.

October 30, 1947

Dear Margie:

I am enclosing you clippings from the papers about your mamma. It looks as if she had gone "Potomac" as all people do who stay in The White House long enough.

When you write to her you must ask her what caused this outburst.

I'm glad she did it. It will make a hit everywhere. She and I are mighty lonesome. Glad to talk with you. Arrangements have been made in Amarillo for Vietta.

Tell your grandma hello and all your Aunts + Uncles too.

Glad you saw your Aunt Mary.

Be a good girl.

YOU OWE ME TWO LETTERS.

Dad

XXXXX
OOOOO

I was on a concert tour of the South and Southwest, and, as you can see from this letter, Dad kept very good track of me.

WASHINGTON, D.C. TO ENGLEWOOD, COLO.

December 3, 1947

My dear Daughter:— I called you last night because I was not sure you were comfortably and properly situated in Des Moines.

You should call your mamma and dad every time you arrive in a town. If you have the Aunt Nat complex you can always reverse the charge. Some day maybe (?) you'll understand what torture it is to be worried about the only person in the world that counts. You should know by now that your dad has only three such persons. Your ma, you and your Aunt Mary. And your Aunt Mary is running around just as you are. So—you see besides all the world and the United States I have a couple of other worries.

Your mamma is going out Thursday with one of your young men. She sent an old bachelor a bunch of flowers—by me!—yesterday afternoon. You'd better get back here and ride herd on her.

I do regret leaving her alone this morning but I have made a date to make an asinine speech in Florida Sat. Dec. 6 and I hope to get some sleep in the meantime. Have had a bad eye but it is on the mend.

Your ma and I shook 1,067 hands last night. The new Marine is a grand looking boy and took the colors out without a stumble.

Tell Fred, Christie + the kids hello.

Lots + lots of love

Dad

In one of his most extraordinary letters, he recounted his
political career from 1940, emphasizing the seeming
inevitability of all that happened.

KEY WEST, FLA. TO WASHINGTON, D.C.

Key West, March 3, 1948

Dear Margie:— It was a very great pleasure to get your
Saturday letter. Will be looking forward to the record you
and Drucie made. Wish I could have gone to the Chocolate
Soldier. Hope they didn't spoil the setting [like] they did the
last time we saw it. Had a beautiful letter from Jeanette
MacDonald. I am enclosing it for you + mother to read. The
gang asked me to invite you and mama to come down with
the mail and have the pleasure of riding back with us. They
hoped you wouldn't hate 'em quite so much if that were
arranged. How about it?

I'm going to give you a record for yourself regarding
these times. It will be a terrible bore, but some time in the
future you may want to know the facts.

You of course know what a terrible campaign the one
of 1940 was. No one thought I could win, including the
President. After the return to the Senate conditions
changed. As you'd know I'd worked just as hard in the first
term as a man could. Held the hearings and put through the
Civil Aeronautics Act; was vice-chairman of the famous
Railroad Hearings and did most of the work which resulted
in the transportation act of 1940; sat on the subcommittee
which held the hearings and wrote the Holding Company
act—the act which stopped the exploitation of public
utilities.

Then came the war. I was a member of the Senate
Appropriations Committee and was on three or four
subcommittees including Military Appropriations. You
remember my twenty-odd-thousand-mile trip to Panama,
every Central American capital and Mexico City in
1939—which also included every port and coast defense

installation in the U.S. You remember my trip just before Christmas 1939 to Puerto Rico and the Virgin Islands on the same mission.

Along in January or late February 1941 I introduced the resolution which created the "Committee to Investigate the National Defense Program" afterward known as the "Truman Committee."

You also know that when the first draft act was passed in 1940 I went to see Gen. Marshall and asked for active service in the Field Artillery. He refused me on account of my age, which was right of course although disappointing to me. Just think of all the trouble you and your mother would have missed had I obtained that assignment!

When camp construction and the immense war purchases began in 1940 I took my old coupe and visited many construction jobs and plants where the government was making purchases. Those visits resulted in the formation of the Special Committee which became so well known.

Jim Byrnes was Chairman of the Committee on Audit + Control of the Senate and was opposed to the formation of the committee. He finally agreed to give me $15,000! I took it. Then asked the Atty. Gen., Robert Jackson (now on the Supreme Court) to recommend his best Asst. for my Counsel. That [is] where Fulton came in. I had to pay him $8,500 per year, which was half the appropriation! Well we went to work and you know the result. Any member of that Committee can tell you how hard your dad worked to make it go as a constructive force for winning the War. It has been said that fifteen billions were saved as were countless scandals prevented. I don't know. Anyway in early 1944 I was voted one of ten men who had made greatest contributions to war effort—the only one from Congress. The vote was taken by fifty press correspondents. Then your pop was picked as one of fifty for statuettes in the National Gallery for contributions to the war effort—the only legislator! Well I guess that Committee did a good job but every member made his contribution and your dad received credit for all of them! Nice work if you can do it. Then came 1944 and that terrible Chicago Convention. I went there to nominate Byrnes. He'd told me that Roosevelt wanted him for Vice-President, and I thought he did. Well I went to see Sidney Hillman, Phil Murray, William Green, Whitney + George Harrison of the R.R. Brotherhoods—each of them told me he was for Wallace but if Wallace couldn't get the nomination that another man would be all right, and each one told me I was the other man. I said to all and sundry that I was not a candidate, would not be and that I was perfectly happy in the Senate.

On Tuesday evening Bob Hannegan came to see me at the Stephens Hotel and told me that Roosevelt wanted me to be the V.P. candidate. I said "no" point blank, and went on working for Byrnes. I was also on the Resolution Committee helping to get a platform together. I reported to Byrnes after each interview exactly what each man said and he said he'd call Roosevelt and let me talk to him. He never succeeded in talking to the President.

Roosevelt was nominated on Thursday and then the real pressure began hammering me to say yes. Finally Hannegan asked me to come over to the Blackstone and listen to a conversation he was to have with Roosevelt in San Diego. That was about 3:30 P.M. central time. Frank Walker, Ed Flynn, Frank Hague and Ed Kelley were there.

Roosevelt's first question of Hannegan was "well have you got that fellow from Missouri lined up?" Bob said no he's very contrary. Then the President said "Well you tell him if he wants to take the responsibility of breaking up the Party in the middle of the war to go ahead and do it." Well that put a new face on things. I scurried to find Bennett Clark to do the nominating. Had trouble getting seconds because every one was pledged by then to someone else. But you were there and know what happened after that.

Late in July I had lunch with the President under the magnolia trees in the White House yard. Talked campaign and he asked me not to fly until after the election! You know about the trip from New Orleans around the west coast, across the Northwest to Chicago, Cleveland, Boston and home. All the old lies were dug up and lots of new ones.

Anyway we won and this is only preliminary to the meat of
what I want to tell you. If there ever was a top secret this is
it. Someday I'll have to tell it. As you know I was
Vice-President from Jan. 20 to April 12, 1945. I was at
Cabinet meetings and saw Roosevelt once or twice in those
months. But he never did talk to me confidentially about the
war, or about foreign affairs or what he had in mind for the
peace after the war.

I had been instrumental in starting the campaign in
the Senate and had spent the summer of 1943 in trying to
sell the country on the famous B^2H^2 resolution which
endorsed the United Nations. I'll tell you someday how B^2H^2
originated. B^2H^2 stands for Ball, Burton, Hatch, Hill. All
Senators at that time and three of them on my Committee!

Well the catastrophe we all dreaded came on April 12
at 4:35 P.M. At 7:09 I was the President and my first decision
was to go ahead with the San Francisco Conference to set up
the U.N.

Then I had to start in reading memorandums, briefs,
and volumes of correspondence on the World situation. Too
bad I hadn't been on the Foreign Affairs Committee or that
F.D.R. hadn't informed me on the situation. I had to find out
about the Atlantic Charter, which by the way does not exist
on paper, the Casablanca meeting, the Montreal meeting,
Tehran meeting, "Yalta," Hull's trip to Moscow, Bretton
Woods, and numerous other things too numerous to
mention. Then Germany folded up. You remember that
celebration that took place on May 8, 1945—my 61st
birthday.

Then came Potsdam. Byrnes, Adm. Leahy, Bohn[?],
interpreter, now Counsel to State Dep't, the present
Ambassador to Italy, Ross and one or two others from the
White House went along. I told Byrnes + Leahy to prepare
an agenda to present to the conference. We worked on it and
had one ready when we arrived at Potsdam.

At Antwerp where we landed from the Augusta I told
Lt. Gen. Lee I'd like to see Harry your cousin. I gave him
Harry's outfit. Well they found him at Glasgow, Scotland
aboard the Queen Elizabeth, asked him if he'd like to see his

uncle and he said he would. They brought him to Potsdam in a plane and I showed him everything. He left for home in three or four days and met his outfit when they landed.

Stalin was a day late, Churchill was on hand when I arrived, I found the Poles in eastern Germany without authority and Russia in possession of East Prussia, Latvia, Estonia and Lithuania, as well as Rumania and Bulgaria. Churchill had urged me to send our troops to the eastern border of Germany and keep them there.

We were about 150 miles east of the border of the occupation zone line agreed to at Yalta. I felt that agreements made in the war to keep Russia fighting should be kept and I kept them to the letter. Perhaps they should not have been adhered to so quickly because later I found the only way to make Russia keep agreements. I did not know that then. Perhaps if we had been slower moving back we could have forced the Russians, Poles, Bulgars, Yugos etc. to behave. But all of us wanted Russia in the Japanese War. Had we known what the Atomic Bomb would do we'd have never have wanted the Bear in the picture. You must remember no tests had been made until several days after I arrived in Berlin.

Adm. Leahy told me that he was an explosives expert and Roosevelt had just thrown $2,600,000,000^{00} away for nothing. He was wrong. But his guess was as good as any. Byrnes thought it might work but he wasn't sure. He thought if it did we would win the Japanese War without much more losses but we still needed the Russians. That was one of my prime objects in going to Berlin—to get to get [sic] the Russians into the Jap War. Well, many agreements were made at Potsdam, the Foreign Minister's Conference was set up, I suggested that the Danube, the Rhine, the Keil[?] Canal, the Black Sea Straits all be made free waterways and that no trade barriers be set up in Europe. The last suggestion got nowhere. Had it been adopted all Europe's and the World's troubles would have been half over.

We entered into agreements for the Government of Germany—not one of which has Russia kept. We made

agreements on China, Korea and other places none of
which has Russia kept. So that now we are faced with
exactly the same situation with which Britain + France
were faced in 1938/39 with Hitler. A totalitarian state is no
different whether you call it Nazi, Fascist, Communist
or Franco's Spain.

Things look black. We've offered control and
disarmament through the U.N., giving up our one
most powerful weapon for the world to control. The Soviets
won't agree. They're upsetting things in Korea, in China, in
Persia (Iran) and in the Near East.

A decision will have to be made. I am going to make it. I
am sorry to have bored you with this. But you've studied
foreign affairs to some extent and I just wanted you to know
your dad as President asked for no territory, no reparations,
no slave laborers—only Peace in the World. We may have to
fight for it. The oligarchy in Russia is no different from the
Czars, Louis XIV, Napoleon, Charles I and Cromwell. It is a
Frankenstein dictatorship worse than any of the others,
Hitler included.

I hope it will end in peace.

Be a nice girl and don't worry about your dad's
worries—but you'll hear all sorts of lies about the things
I've told you—these are the facts.

I went to Potsdam with the kindliest feeling toward
Russia—in a year and a half they cured me of it.

Lots of love
Dad

Here is a letter Dad sent me from Winston Churchill, along with Dad's reply.

Margie:—

　　Here is a real souvenir for your scrapbook—two personal letters from "Winston"

Dad

[enclosed: 1 letter, 3 envelopes, 1 package label, and copy of return letter to W.C. from H.S.T.]

| Private | 7 June 1948 |
| Westerham 93 | Chartwell, Westerham, Kent |

My dear Harry,

　　Thank you so much for y'r letter and for sweeping away so many tiresome obstacles. I am really v'y much obliged to you.

　　I think a g't deal about you + y'r affairs—or 'our' affairs as they sh'd be called. I am not j [?] from [?] about this autumn. If the U.S. will be much stronger actually + relatively next year than this (thanks to y'r provision), they may ask themselves in the Kremlin whether the Soviets will not be worse off + weaker. This is always a dangerous conjuncture[?]. However we must all do our best without fear or flinching.

　　I greatly admire y'r conduct of International Affairs in Europe during the tenure of the most powerful office in the world. I really wish I c'd have been some help.

Winston S. Churchill

P.S. How I wish we c'd have another good talk— + even another game!

"Copy" July 10, 1948

My dear Winston:—

I was deeply touched by your good letter of June 7. I am going through a terrible political "trial by fire." Too bad it must happen at this time.

Your great country and mine are founded on the fact that the people have the right to express themselves on their leaders, no matter what the crisis.

Your note accompanying The Gathering Storm is highly appreciated, and I have made it a part of the book.

We are in the midst of grave and trying times. You can look with satisfaction on your great contribution to the overthrow of Nazism + Fascism in the world.

"Communism"—so-called, is our next great problem. I hope we can solve it without the "blood and tears" the other two cost.

May God bless and protect you.
Ever sincerely your friend

Harry Truman

Thanks, "a million" for The Gathering Storm.

*In this letter he combined his knowledge that I was painting
the kitchen pantry with his worries about Congress.*

WASHINGTON, D.C. TO INDEPENDENCE, MO.

July 28, 1948

Dear Margie:— I was highly pleased to get your nice letter.
And more than glad to get the telegram from you and your
mother about the message to Congress.

You seem to have been slaving away at your paint job
and your garden. I am hoping to see an excellent result in
each instance. I shall expect to be able to pick a nice
bouquet from the garden when I come home Sunday
and I shall hope to be able to see myself in those slick
pantry walls!

I am somewhat exhausted myself getting ready for this
terrible Congress. They are in the most turmoil any
Congress I can remember ever has been. Some of them want
to quit right away, some of them want to give the Dixiecrats
a chance to filibuster and the Majority are very anxious to
put the Pres. in the hole if they can manage it.

It will take a few days for the message to sink in
completely.

In the meantime I shall take it easy and let 'em sweat.

I'm going down the Potomac tomorrow and stay until
Saturday at 10:00 A.M. Then to New York and then to K.C.
Should arrive at 7:00 P.M. if present plans hold. That is P.M.
Saturday. I'll stay for the election and come back Wednesday
A.M.

Tell Mama I'm bringing a turkey, can bring two if you
want 'em.

Be a nice girl + keep working hard. It's good for the
body and helps the soul too. Lots of love

Dad

XXXXXXX
OOOOOO

Most of this letter is self-explanatory, although the first part refers to a Saturday Evening Post *article titled "Why Shouldn't I Sing?" and the end refers to a trip Dad was planning to take to Washington to dedicate the Grand Coulee dam on May 11th.*

EGLIN AIR FORCE BASE, FLA. TO WASHINGTON, D.C.

April 22, 1950

Dear Margie:— I have just finished another reading of the article in today's <u>Saturday Evening Post</u>. It is a very good statement of the facts—made in such a way as to offend no one—not even your very touchy family on both sides! I really don't see how you ever succeeded in getting the terrible anti-Truman <u>Post</u> to publish the facts as they are. Next to Mr. Clare Boothe Luce and his slick paper weeklies and <u>Fortune</u> there's not a nastier publication in the country than old Ben Franklin's <u>Post</u>. Of course, Ben wouldn't recognize the dirty "royalist" sheet that goes under the name of the paper he started.

But it circulates among Gallup Pollsters and members of the Chamber of Commerce and the Manufacturer's Assn. along with the members of the Chicago Board of Trade, N.Y. Stock Exchange and Real Estate Boards, so some closed mind people will learn something from it. It's a grand piece.

I hope you'll continue to the top of your profession and attain "<u>everything</u>" you want. I'm sure you will do that. For some reason you know and have learned that hard work and honesty of purpose really bring results. Just remember that you have at least one person who'll back you to the limit and who'll stay by you whether you are up or down. He may be and probably is some what of a handicap now but that will end someday and you can then be on your own. You'd have won anyway so don't let the White House worry you. And don't ever be an Alice Roosevelt or a Margaret Wilson whatever you do.

I think you, your mother and I will have a grand trip next month without the handicap of the one in 1948. The opposition seems to be scared stiff over what your dad will do on that trip and I'm going to fool' em as usual. It will be a dignified really non-political performance for the benefit of our foreign program.

Take care of yourself and keep on working. Good luck and lots of love

Dad

P.S. It's 4:00 A.M.! I went to bed at 10:30 believe it or not. There's an S.S. man under both my windows. I heard 'em cough.

The whole family (mostly mother's side) on the *Williamsburg*.

In this letter, he gave me a lesson about the importance of a man's word.

WASHINGTON, D.C. TO NEW YORK CITY

June 6, 1950

Dear Margie:— I talked with Mr. Bass last night and was not impressed with his attitude. He informed me that he wanted your contracted agreement with Mr. Davidson canceled or he would see to it that Miss Trauble would display no more interest in you. It's a good thing he was not at my desk.

With much effort I remained calm and polite. But I did tell him that when a Truman signed an agreement or made one by word of mouth, that agreement would be kept come hell or high water.

You must not act impulsively for anyone. It is doubly necessary that you do the right thing.

The contract as you know was entirely rewritten at my suggestion and it is a good one. You have done well under it and it seems to me Mr. Davidson has tried to do right.

I am appreciative of Miss Trauble's interest in you and I know you are, but neither of us should stand for an out and out blackmail proposition to satisfy an undoubted prejudice of a third party who had nothing to do with your contractual relationship with Davidson.

You should inform yourself of both sides, bearing in mind that your contract with Davidson was voluntary on your part and that you met Miss Trauble as a result of that contract with Davidson.

All I'm asking you to do is to weigh the facts, act in your own future interest and bear in mind that there are dozens of excellent voice coaches. My only interest is yours.

Lots of love   Dad

Despite all of his aggravations with Congress, he at least found some pleasure in my acting as "a great ambassador of goodwill."

WASHINGTON, D.C. TO PARIS, FRANCE

June 19, 1951

Dear Margie: Your cable arrived Sunday after our telephone talk. It was most highly appreciated.

Your postscript from The Hague came yesterday in the pouch but the letter to which it is a postscript has not arrived! I guess the letter will come today. You handled the conversation with the Queen of Holland about the proposed visit of herself and the Prince Consort perfectly. I'm hoping they'll wait until we are settled in the rehabilitated White House before they come.

I sent you a copy of this week's Life by Mr. Harriman. Mr. Loose seems to have given you a fair shake—but wait, it won't last. Your press over here has been excellent. You are making a great ambassador of goodwill.

You may have to walk home if this strike continues. I'm hoping for a settlement this week.

The President of Ecuador comes to town tomorrow for the usual round, tea at 4:00 P.M., dinner at 8 at the Carlton and his dinner at the Statler on Friday. Then he'll tell me what he wants, go to N.Y. and then back home. I hope we can get him home safely. I'm always worried when these heads of State come to town until they are safely at home again.

Congress is acting up terribly. No appropriations to date. Democrats acting perfect demagogues. Republicans acting as usual. They are about to sabotage my whole five-year peace plan but I guess we'll survive it.

Your mother is fine. Talked to her last night and every one is all right.

Take care of yourself and have a good time.

Lots of love

Dad

Harry Truman to Margaret Truman

Post-Presidential Years (1955–63)

This is the first note I received from him after he was President.

KANSAS CITY, MO. TO NEW YORK CITY

17 October 1955

re: pictures and: "Your mother is moaning because she sits at home so much but I'll remedy that!"

Christmas dinner 1947 at the White House with the family.

*He wrote this letter after one of my first television
appearances.*

KANSAS CITY, MO. TO NEW YORK CITY

October 18, 1955

Dear Margie: — Just read the <u>Times</u> about your show. The
old man is as pleased as "punch." If it is what you want to do
of course that would be what your old dad wants.

We—your mama and I, were so pleased to see you that
your ma took a good picture. Now that's really something.

The Woodwards come today at 1:58 P.M. if the plane's on
time. Last night we had dinner with Randall Jessee at his
house. Dave Garroway and, of all people, Thomas Hart
Benton were there. It seems that Tom Benton thinks your
pa is a top-notch president. It made me ashamed of my
opinion of him as a mural painter.

I went down to the Union Station at 6:15 and said a few
words for Dave Garroway and told him he'd now have
competition from a very competent young lady. He said, "No
competition from me."

Just remember if there is anything that pop can do for
you say what it is. Your mother + I hope you can come
home as soon as possible.

Love
Dad

Even at this late date, Dad was still complaining about my not writing him and rejected my excuse of poor handwriting.

KANSAS CITY, MO. TO NEW YORK CITY

December 5, 1955

Dear Margie:

I am enclosing you a letter to Burt Bacharach which you can give to him.

I don't like the last sentence in your letter. All I am interested in is to have you write so the customers can read it. Of course, you inherit handwriting from both your mother and your dad that is individual and not very legible but I like to look at it anyway.

The trip west was a magnificent success—much better than anybody anticipated—and the appearance in St. Louis before the four thousand Catholic young people was just out of this world. The Archbishop, all the Bishops and Monsignors who were in charge of the program were highly pleased with what happened and that was what I was hoping to accomplish.

With love,
Dad

The reviews from abroad came this morning. Thanks. They sure are good. If you knew how much I like to look at that scrawl of yours, you'd send one oftener.

He sent me this letter after my first book, Souvenir, *came out.*

                                          February 20, 1956

Dear Margie:

Here's the first letter about your book.
I'm enclosing it, together with a copy of my reply.

                                                  Love,
                                                  Dad

Read the installment in Good Housekeeping—my, what an
emotional old man your dad is! He really didn't know that
he is that good! He ain't.

A snapshot I took of Mother and Dad in Blair House garden.

In this letter, Dad gave me a lecture about trusting people.

KANSAS CITY, MO. TO NEW YORK CITY

March 19, 1956

Dear Margie:— Your pop was overcome almost—well, as
nearly as he ever is—when you and Cliff came to the plane
in that storm. That leaky roof interview turned out
perfectly too. Your young man impresses me the more I see
of him. He has common sense and that can't be acquired.

The trip to Scranton was an overwhelming
success and the trip home was without incident. Your
mama met me with Mike in <u>my</u> car. She said hers was so
dirty she was afraid I wouldn't ride in it. I'd just had it
washed and polished it myself a day or two before I went
east.

I have just talked to Sam Rayburn. His nephew (52)
died on the operating table and his widowed sister-in-law,
the mother of the nephew, fell dead when the doctor told
her of her son's death. Miss Lou has been under the knife
for cancer and nothing can be done.

But Sam is taking it all in stride as the great man he is
should. He told me if he had a daughter he'd be as happy as I
should be, and am, over your affair. He also told me that if
he wasn't invited to the wedding you would be barred from
calling him Uncle Sam and grandpa. So you'd better do
something about that.

There's one thing that worried me in our phone
conversation last night. You said no one is to be trusted.
Maybe your dad, who has had more contracts and
experiences with people than anyone alive, [can] tell you
that more than 95% of all the people can be trusted.

If you don't trust the people you love and those who
work for you in all capacities you'll be the unhappiest and
[most] frustrated person alive.

Think of the immense number of people I've had under me—County Court, Senate, V.P. and President of the United States. I had two no-goods in the County setup, one in the Senate and only two in the Cabinet, only two on the staff. Now the good ones added up to several hundred.

I believe in our constitutional, common-law background—that no person is guilty until it's proven. The Corpus Juris of Justinian and the Code Napoleon work from the premise that everyone is guilty until he proves his innocence. Justinian's empire is gone—so is Napoleon's and the successor to it. Well, think about it baby.

Your dad loves you and wants you to be happy—you can't be unless you trust and have faith in people.

Dad

Mother, Aunt Natalie, Aunt May and Uncle Frank playing bridge in the family quarters in the White House, 1952.

This was my father's first trip to Europe as a private citizen.

LONDON, ENGLAND, TO NEW YORK CITY

June 22, 1956

Dear Margie + Clif:

That Oxford degree was very impressive and a most
dignified affair. A lady, Dame Lillian Penson, and I headed
the honor section of the parade. Someone called her Mrs.
Truman along the march and she very carefully and
forcefully informed whoever it was that she is who she is
and that her first name was spelled with three L's. I told her
that [I] hoped the papers wouldn't get all three of them in
the middle or at the end of her name. She is a great educator
with a good sense of humor. We had a good time on the
march in and out. She said she never had an idea what it
meant to meet twenty or thirty photographers all at once
and I told her Mr. Clare Boothe Luce had had the same
experience in Rome. But I also told her that no discourtesy
was intended by mentioning him. She almost lost her
beefeater hat on that one.

I had a chance to meet and talk to David Posner at the
garden party after the degree ceremony was over. His poem,
parts of which he read from a pulpit on my right, was really
great and understandable. When I told him that my
son-in-law had called him to my attention he was highly
pleased. He seems to be a nice young man. His father was at
the ceremony and the garden party.

That staid, stiff Oxford audience gave me a political-
convention ovation. Lord Halifax told me afterward it had
never happened before. They took me to their gaudy dinner
that night and the same thing happened and it was worse
or better, however you look at it, last night at the Pilgrims'
dinner. It took two Lords and a Prime Minister to introduce
me and the Foreign Secretary to thank me for my speech
and they say these British are not demonstrative!

Had a grand trip to the Commons after a luncheon with the Speaker. I got him to tell me all about his powers and duties and how "Speaker" originated. He told me, in the time of Charles I + II that the man who went to the King spoke for the Parliament and sometimes lost his head for doing it. So when a Speaker for the Commons is elected he has to put on a show of resistance when he's escorted to the presiding officer's chair to save his head! I saw the death warrant of Charles I, the orders of Elizabeth I and Henry VIII proroguing Parliament and the Charles I bill of rights which the Librarian of the House of Lords tried to tell me is more important than the Magna Carta and our Declaration. Then he told me that Charles repudiated and when I told him that annulled it he said yes but he lost his head. But Cromwell didn't implement it and was afterwards dug up and lost his head too. He changed the subject and said the beheading of a dead man was gruesome. I wonder about a live one.

Thanks for the Persian article, wish I could go there. Hope all's well with you both. Clif, you are a much better correspondent than skinny.

We'll see you July 3 and how glad we'll be to do that.

Your ma sends love too!

Dad

This was Dad's first letter to his son-in-law, my husband, Clifton Daniel.

KANSAS CITY, MO. TO ?

July 27, 1956

Dear Clif:

I am sorry I have been such a long time in telling you how very much I appreciated your sending me a copy of the speech you made at Colgate University and the articles by James Reston. Your letter has just now come to the top of the tremendous accumulation of mail I've been trying to work through ever since my return from Europe. We had to have an extra girl in all last week to help out.

That statement of yours on Russia is the best I've ever seen.

Sincerely yours,
DAD Truman

Tell Margie to behave herself and don't give her too much rope!

I still have this key ring with the battleship Missouri *on it.*

KANSAS CITY, MO. TO ?

October 5, 1956

Dear Margaret:

Here is a key ring with the Battleship <u>Missouri</u> on it. I thought you would like to have it. I also have one, so we are together on it. I am sorry the situation was such that I did not get to see as much of you and Clif as I wanted to while I was in New York, but I guess that is the condition under which I have to live.

I know your mother enjoyed her visit to no end.

I am hoping we will have a grand time at Christmas.

Love,
Dad

Tell Clif those <u>N.Y. Times</u> articles on the situation are fair and excellent.

Dad was referring to the Bible on which he was sworn. He
had given it to me but I thought he should have it back. He
felt I had made the right decision in returning it to him.

KANSAS CITY, MO. TO NEW YORK CITY

April 15, 1957

Dear Margie:— I'm so glad the birthday money was useful.
That silver chest and dressing gown are things your dad
never could have thought of or even found out about.

I know you've had a most pleasant visit with Mr. +
Mrs. Daniel. They are people of good judgment and
common sense—and so is their son.

Your idea about that Bible is surely the proper one. I
had hoped that you would do just what you suggest. But I
gave you the book and it is yours to do with as you please.
You've made the right decision. I'll bring it back when we
come in May. If you insist, we'll stay with you.

We'll arrive May 1 and leave the morning of May 3 if
my plans hold out.

Maybe the Carlyle will let me hold forth over there on
the morning of the 2nd and I won't have to muddy up your
apartment.

I've never had a nicer letter from [anyone] but your ma
on rare occasions.

Be a nice girl. Lots of love

Dad

My Aunt Mary went out and bought a television so she could see me on TV. (She was the last family holdout for buying a TV set!)

INDEPENDENCE, MO. TO NEW YORK CITY

January 2, 1958

Dear Margie + Clif—and "Buster" or "That"!

Your Aunt Mary went and bought a television set for no other purpose than to see some TV shows we are all interested in. What she wants is to be informed when one of those shows is on. Do it will you, so I won't get scolded.

Your ma is getting better—you know how to tell about that. What a way to spend New Year's Day! In bed with the old man sitting in a rocking chair looking at her and grinning most of the time. She didn't like my bringing in the Doc but that's what she needed.

Don't forget Aunt Mary!

Lots of love to all of you

Dad

In 1958, he was still no fonder of the Kansas City Star
than he had been earlier.

? TO ?

January 28, 1958

Dear Margie + Clif:—

Here is a clipping (enclosed) from the dirty old Star
about the sale of the rest of the old home. It was sold for
$220,000.00 of which $55,000.00 goes for tax! But I have a
note for $180,000.00 at 4½% for five years so I guess your
ma and me can eat anyway.

In Sunday's Star they published air pictures of old Bill
Nelson's Gallery, a farm at Blue Springs and no Library.

Your mother + I are going to the Nelson Gallery to see
some of Churchill's pictures on Thursday at 5:15 and then
to dinner with Doc Sam Roberts and an ear expert. Dr. Sam
as you know is a Republican but he spent several days at
Research telling Doc Wallis what he should do to keep me
alive—so I guess I can trust him with a dead ear.

I sure hope that you and Clif will come to Washington.
Should I make a Mayflower reservation? I've made one for
Sam + Dorothy for the 20th. I am having a party for all my
former staff and their wives and you're both invited. It will
take place at noon on Feb. 20th if my plans work out.

Love to you both—give that tough kid a kiss.

Dad
+
Grandad

Although Dad's political prognostications were usually right on target, his assessment of Jack Kennedy's chances turned out to be completely wrong.

INDEPENDENCE, MO. TO NEW YORK CITY

July 9, 1960

Dear Margie:— Your note of the 4th cost my vest and shirt two buttons' space. Of course your dad's as proud as Punch of your two boys. If someone had been thoughtful enough to hand Kiffie up to me for the other arm we'd have had no difficulty—and no pictures!

I couldn't lean over to pick him up with the other boy holding me down or up.

Looks like I'm in a hell of a fix as regards the Dem. Convention. Old man Joe Kennedy has spent over 4 million dollars to buy the nomination for his son!

Then the anti-pope and the Lutherans, Baptists and Methodists, with the Presbyterians and the Campbellites will beat him. Love from,   Dad

Dad sent some stamps that he had received to my third son.

INDEPENDENCE, MO. TO NEW YORK CITY

March 27, 1963

Dear Margie:

Enclosed are some stamps which a Mr. French in San Francisco sent me for the new grandson "Harrison Gates."

Thought you would like to add these to your collection.

Love,
Dad

Hope all's well. Understand that "Grandma" put one over and called you without me.

The whole family at Christmas dinner, 1952.

This was his final letter to me and it was written after his last operation. It was typical of him that he found canceling his appointments more painful than his operation.

INDEPENDENCE, MO. TO NEW YORK CITY

April 30, 1963

Dear Margie:—

Here is another job for you if you want to do it.
You don't have to do it if it isn't convenient.
I am slowly and gradually getting over my upset. For the first time in my life I really passed out. Your mother was suspicious but her suspicions had no foundation in fact. That knifing I had was worse than I thought. I've canceled all dates until July 31st or August 15th.
That hurts worse than the knife did!

Lots of love
                         Dad

Margaret Truman
to Harry Truman

THE following are a few of my letters to Dad. When I reread them now, they seem far removed from the matters with which he had to deal in those cataclysmic days.

My political statements were limited to votes of support (as when I excitedly wrote him on June 14, 1946, that "I've registered to vote now and you have mine"); facetious remarks (as on December 19, 1946, when I told him to "be good and don't let the country go to pot"); pep talks (as on August 25, 1951, when I told him to "give it to 'em on Sept. 1st and show everybody who's still on top and in control of the situation"); and my no-holds-barred opinions on his appointments ("I believe your Ambassador in Stockholm is about as stupid and pompous an ass as I have ever seen").

Maybe he was glad not to have to read about politics. (But he would not have been happy about my using that three-letter word, since members of our family generally did not use that type of language in front of one another, with the occasional "hell" or "damn" from my mother.) He was always happy to hear news about my career, or to go along with our game about the White House ghost (which we all liked to make believe existed, even though we knew better), or to be filled in on gossip concerning our family and friends, or even to hear me apologize about so rarely writing him back.

Dad really didn't care what I wrote him; it was simply that I wrote him which mattered to him. I'm glad to have returned at least some pleasure to someone who gave me so much of it.

INDEPENDENCE, MO. TO WASHINGTON, D.C. — POSTMARKED
3 SEPTEMBER 1945

Sunday
noon

Dear Daddy,

Annette and I have just come back from church. We nearly blew to pieces as a wind is blowing up a gale. It's a gorgeous sunny day but some wind!

We have been having a grand time. Last night Annette went to a show with Shawsie + Tish, and I had a dinner date with Pymen Crow. He's a Lieutenant in the Navy, a flyer. We had a good dinner and danced.

Today we're going to take the guests for a drive thru the famous county of Jackson. (on your roads)

I haven't packed at all yet so I may be on the train Sat. morning and I may not. Anyway Mother won't take up as much room as she usually does and I can have the trunk so it won't be hard cause for once I'll have enough room.

The rest of this week is going to be hectic and Annette and I haven't had much sleep. We are going to have even less.

We'll see you Sat. morning and move back into <u>that</u> <u>House</u>! It'll be nice to see my poppy again for a longer while than this summer.

Loads of love,
Margie

XXXXXXXXXX
OOOOOOOOOO

ABOARD TRAIN TO WASHINGTON, D.C.—POSTMARKED 23
SEPTEMBER 1945

Wednesday
somewhere in Illinois between
Vincennes and St. Louis

Dear Daddy,

This is written en route and will probably go up and
down the page as the train goes around the curves. We had a
rough night last night, more so than usual when they
attached the engine on going over the mountains. I felt like
a cocktail must feel when you shake it up and down, in the
upper berth. The engine on the back huffed when the one in
front puffed and they never did get together and we were in
the middle! Mother and Grandmother had breakfast in the
drawing room (Plutocrats!) but they didn't order for Pete
and me so we waded through snow drifts (between the
cars) and ate breakfast in the dining car. We hadn't
intended to eat breakfast at all, and had decided to get up
just in time for early lunch on the B + O but we both forgot
about the change in time and darned if I didn't get up and
get dressed before I thought about it! It was only 10 o'clock
instead of 11, phooey! So now we have to eat lunch too on
the Mop. Nuts!

The snow is pretty deep between Vincennes and St.
Louis and there is ice on the outside of the train windows.
The sun is out though so it'll probably all melt just in time
for Christmas.

Mr. (Attorney-General) Tom Clark was in the
compartment on the other side of Mother's drawing room.
He was on his way to Cinncinati (I can't spell that) to make
a speech to the Bar Association there. He very nicely offered
to do anything he could for us, but we all went to bed right
after we got on so we didn't need anything. He's the member
of your Inner Circle who's got the Pi Phi wife, good man to

have around. Mr. Nicholson is on the other side of Pete +
me, so we all had the whole car. Be good and don't forget
Mother's bags when you come!

XXXXXXX   Loads of love
OOOOOOO   "Sistie"

[on outer sheet of paper: This is cause you can read it on the
  outside of the envelope cause the envelopes are so thin.
                                                      M.]

KANSAS CITY, MO. TO WASHINGTON, D.C. — POSTMARKED
9 JUNE 1946

Saturday
8:20 C.S.T.

Dear Daddy,

We are coming into Jeff City and the Mop is swaying back and forth, although it's not as rough as the B + O was last night. We have had a very good trip. Aunt Nat has about frozen Beuf and me with the air-conditioning as she is very hot because the thermometer in St. Louis said 95°. We have all been sleeping and the foursome has played some bridge. They got me in one game and were they sorry about that!

Am hoping to go to church tomorrow but we get in awful late tonight. Will mail this tomorrow.

XXXXX   Gobs of love
OOOOO   "Sistie"

INDEPENDENCE, MO. TO WASHINGTON, D.C. — POSTMARKED
14 JUNE 1946

> Friday
> (really Thursday
> at 10:20)

Dear Daddy,

Your letter came this morning and this is to prove my
arm isn't broken. Yesterday I sent you an album of Mozart
that we liked at the Symphony concert for Papa's Day which
in case you didn't know is on this Sunday. I guess I'll have to
admit you're the world's nicest and best Dad. (I am not out
of funds, that's free.) I hope you like the records. If they're
broken in any way let me know as Jenkins will replace it.

Aunt Mary is home and Mamma Truman is back in her
own home safe and sound. Also we'll get Harry a wedding
present. I didn't even know he'd gotten married. I thought it
was to be later in the month. I've heard she's a nice girl, and
he's a nice boy even if he is my cousin so they should be
happy. It will be good to know another Harry Truman is
living on and taking care of the old farm, won't it?

We haven't been doing anything much and that's
wonderful. It's cool here tonight. Mother and I went to K.C.
today and took Mrs. Donephy (P.E.O) to lunch. One
saleswoman stopped in while we were shopping and said
your labor speech made a vote for the Dems. from her.

Beuf and I are going to a movie tomorrow and Shawsie
and I are having lunch on Saturday. I have a voice lesson on
Sat. Got to get back to work and get somewhere. I have been
reading a Shakespeare play a nite, so far am reading the
historical ones first, in sequence. It makes me so mad, here
I am out of school and I can't stay away from "learning." Be
good and be tough. I've registered to vote now and you have
mine.

XXXXXXXXXX   Loads of love,
OOOOOOOO   "Sistie"

INDEPENDENCE, MO. TO WASHINGTON, D.C.—POSTMARKED
13 AUGUST 1946

Monday

Dear Daddy,

Thank you very much for the very nice letter. Thank
you also for the big piece of green lettuce. I'll use it
sparingly.

I have been singing all afternoon with Mrs. Strickler,
Mrs. Shaw at the piano and Mr. Letson, Rose Conway's
uncle, is Rigoletto in that opera. We're getting it polished up
so I'll be able if I get the chance to stand on the Met stage
and sing it as if I'd always been there singing opera. It's not
so hard when you get the hang of it, and it's loads of fun.
We're going to work every day this week.

Went to a picnic at Louise Duke's last night. Tish and
her husband and Wiley Mitchell, one of Louise's cousins. We
had a lot of fun. I guess I was a bad girl, because I made the
date last week and Cousin Ethel didn't know about the
family gathering until Sunday morning. Aunt Louella never
did call us so I felt I had to go to Tish's. Mother said they had
a good time seeing the Texas cousins. We took Aunt Mary's
presents to her all right so don't worry.

Wednesday night the Stricklers are coming for dinner.
It's her birthday.

Nothing much has happened since you left. The town
has been sleeping off all the excitement you caused. Did you
see Time this week about George Allen? It's a riot.

Pete says dinner is ready so guess I'd better go. After
singing all afternoon I'm so hungry. Bet I'll get fat now, and
I don't want to. Be good and sleep lots on the boat.

Loads of love,
"Sistie"
XXXXXXX
OOOOOOO

INDEPENDENCE, MO. TO WASHINGTON, D.C. —POSTMARKED
11 SEPTEMBER 1946

Tuesday

Dear Daddy,

The sweaters and the plaid material are super. I am
going to have Mr. Lindsay here make me a skirt and a
short jacket out of the material. There is plenty if I don't
gain any more. The sweaters are so soft and fit just
perfectly. You did right well by the old lady and me I'd say.

Fred Truman went to the hospital to have his appendix
out. It wasn't sudden, he'd had it for some time and Dr.
thought he'd better get it before it got acute or something.
Guess Uncle V. has told you all about it.

You better lock your door and prop up some chairs and
next time you hear knocks don't answer it'll probably be A.
Jackson in person.

I have been working very hard and have about finished
Lucia and am working on Lakené[?]. It is really hard, much
harder than Rigoletto or Lucia. I hope you won't mind too
much if I do stay here until October. It seems the best way to
be sure of singing the right way. I almost have it so I can do
it without Mrs. S. and that's her object as she can't always
be with me when I sing.

Be good and watch those ghosts!
XXXXXXX   Loads of love,
OOOOOOO   "Sistie"

ABOARD THE BALTIMORE AND OHIO TO WASHINGTON,
D.C.—POSTMARKED 19 DECEMBER 1946

Thursday

Dear Daddy,

This is a little confusing trying to write and keep the pen and paper right side up. It has been a very smooth trip so far and I had a lower! It was much more comfortable than the one next to the dining room.

Reathel[?] just got off and her brother met her. She seemed to be glad to get home. Mitchell has some chocolate ice cream for me and I hope it's more chocolate than last time, as it was a rather odd color since she'd never made it before, but no matter what it looks like I'll eat it because she went to so much trouble to make it.

Mrs. Sonter is getting on at St. Louis so I guess that will curtail all naps. Not much so far has happened as I didn't get up until time for lunch.

We seem to be pulling into the outskirts of St. L. so guess I'd better finish this off so Mr. Dorsey can mail it with Mother's.

Now you come home soon please, <u>before</u> Christmas Day. Be good and don't let the country go to pot.

XXXXXX   Loads of love
OOOOOO   "Sistie"

INDEPENDENCE, MO. TO WASHINGTON, D.C. —POSTMARKED
11 JULY 1947

Friday

Dear "foolish young" Daddy,

I am a lazy bad girl and haven't put a pen anywhere
near paper since I got home. So here goes, I'll see if I can
still write. I received your letter with the oil well in it and I
am completely at sea. I've never seen anything like it. It is
really wonderful, but you should have it not me. I'll put it
away in my bank account and keep it for you. How do I
write to Mr. Helm? And is that his wife's name on it?

Mother and Grandmother are going to Denver on
Monday and I am going to my two ancient aunts. The food
will undoubtedly put on more pounds. We have been going
to Blue Springs as it is. I am working every day, and I
may have to wait until October before I start, in order to get
the best dates, and the weather and all will be better. I have
cleared everything up with Admiral Holloway at the
Academy and if I go there it will be a special concert. I'll
write him again when plans are definite. Mamma T. looks
very good and we'll see her on Sunday. I'll write again <u>soon</u>.

Loads of love
XXXXXX   Margie
OOOOOO

INDEPENDENCE, MO. TO WASHINGTON, D.C.—POSTMARKED
21 JULY 1947

Monday

Dear Daddy,

Thank you for your nice letter, but don't you go getting up at 4:00 A.M. to write me. I'd collapse if anyone suggested such a thing. I'm glad to have the Yuan 5¢ piece. Have just had a long lesson at the Music Hall and am tired. That tour better be good to be worth all this work. But then I've been told that everything worthwhile requires hard work.

I am glad to have Bessie back since I was tired of commuting between three houses. She had a nice visit, but was ready to get back since I don't think she got much real rest. Of course she didn't get any here this morning and neither did I. Lucy called at the ungodly hour of 8:30 there. Louise called from London and it took two hours for the operator to find her. She must have missed looking in the cocktail lounge. Then Nancy from B   's[?] came to hang curtains and mother was taking them down at the same time in my room in back. Such a day. Just when I get back to sleep blooie! it was time to get up and go for a lesson. You come home soon and be good.

Loads of love
XXXXX OOOOO Sistie

INDEPENDENCE, MO. TO WASHINGTON, D.C. —POSTMARKED
25 JULY 1947

Friday
1:00 A.M.
(better than 4:00 A.M.)

Dear Daddy,

I've been keeping up with you in the paper. You must
have had a good visit in the Senate. Hope no lousy Rep. (or
Fulbright) is sitting in your seat.

We drove out to the Drive-In Theater at 40 and Noland
to see <u>My Darling Clementine</u>—phooey, we couldn't even see
it, the film was so dark, and what we did see I guess we
didn't miss much.

Beuf and I have been playing badminton every night
and in sweaters! It's so cold I'm almost blue. I have the
heater on in my room tonight as I washed my hair and it's
better. We're sleeping under two blankets.

Things are rather slow around here, and all the men
look like they belong in that movie. They all look like a
bunch of thugs. Thank goodness I didn't live in the days
when men wore beards.

Mamma T. as you know is having a little bit of a rugged
time, but I know her and I'm sure she'll be all right. Be
good, and hurry home.

Loads of love,
Margie

INDEPENDENCE, MO. TO WASHINGTON, D.C.—POSTMARKED
26 SEPTEMBER 1947

Friday

Dear Daddy,

Everything is so quiet, no salutes being fired and
no champaign [sic] to drink. I am back in the harness and
working hard every day. I am sorry I missed talking to you.
Beuf and I were in a hot and I mean hot and fast game of
double solitaire. I won by one point. She and mother, and I
are going to K.C. tomorrow to see about getting the [?] for
the stones. Aunt Mary was delighted with hers and I have it
here to take tomorrow too. She saw it and decided to have
hers fixed something like ours, each one will probably have
to be set a little differently.

We haven't gotten to Blue Springs yet as it's been pretty
chilly, but it's supposed to get warm Sat. so we'll go there. I
sent Capt. Dennison two record Albums today that he
doesn't have, one the "little night music" of Mozart and a
new Liszt concerto recorded by Rubinstein and the
San Antonio Orchestra.

The Santa-Cali-San almost wrecked the town I'm told
and most of the ffi's (first families of Indep.) stayed home to
avoid the mobs on the square. The stores all had a run on
shaving lotion + cream the day after.

Be good and don't let the Ruskies bother you.

Lots of love   Mother has all her windows up
                 and I'm freezing so will quit and
                 go to bed

XXXXX   Sistie

Saturday

Dear Daddy,

Mother and I have been painting like mad and have
finished the china closet. It is a pretty shade of green, but oh
my! the work.

I went to Ann Louise's for lunch which Cousin Annie
fixed so it was but good. Cousin Gates wanted me to tell you
that the grain + corn crop is phenomenal and all up +
down the Midwest and nothing can stop it now even a flood
or 2 because it's well over 25% more, he said, than ever
before. He said it'll take care of food prices, I suppose you
know that, but he wanted me to tell you the farmers are
happy, darn 'em they ought to be. I'd like to have seen the
brawl between Wallace and Pegler[?]. P. had a riotous article
about W. in tonight's Star. I have weeded and transplanted
in my garden 'til I'm exhausted.

See you Sunday, and be sure you get here.

Loads of love,

"Sistie"

INDEPENDENCE, MO. TO WASHINGTON, D.C. —POSTMARKED
22 AUGUST 1948

Saturday
But late!

Dear Daddy,

It is really H-O-T out here. Has been to 100° nearly
every day for about five days. Dashed out to lunch and
tonight we had a picnic in the backyard and had an electric
fan out there to stir up a breeze. My zinnias are way up and
the marigolds and bachelor's buttons have bloomed. I have
finished 3/4 of the kitchen with the second coat and it looks
good. I'll finish it tomorrow afternoon I hope.

Have some more good swims and be good. I can check
up on you in the paper.

XXXXXX   Lots of love
OOOOOO   "Sistie"

Dear Daddy,

We have had a nice trip, only rough one day and that wasn't bad. I like the ship to roll some so I know I'm not on dry land. Everyone on board in the crew has been very considerate and has left me alone.

Have heard from Mr. Gifford and I am taking the boat train to London. Just think I'll be in London oh boy! Had a cable from the Eisenhowers and I'll see them in Paris.

Played Bingo tonight and didn't win a cent. There are some nice people at the Captain's table. One young man is Ronald Egan, whose father you met, he was Pres. of Western Union before he died. Ron is to take over the office in London and some in France and Switzerland. Another used to live in K.C. he's in Western Union too. Diana Churchill Sandys is there too. Annette and I play ping pong every day. It's strange to hit a ball and have the ship roll and the ball doesn't go over the net.

I'll cable you from London. Will you tell Mother every time I cable when you talk to her please? Then I'll send only one to you or to her and not two. I have discovered they do not grow on trees. I'm off to do my best to make you proud of me.

Lots of love
Baby

OSLO, NORWAY TO WASHINGTON, D.C. — POSTMARKED 25
AUGUST 1951

Helsinki
+
Oslo

Dear Daddy,

Now I am making a valiant effort to keep my temper
under control and I have simmered down somewhat! I
believe your Ambassador in Stockholm is about as stupid
and pompous an ass as I have ever seen. Having a man with
so little mental poise in a position of trust like that is
frightening. I am speaking of course of that silly incident
involving the S.S. boys. I didn't get exercised over it
until Butterworth tried to throw them to the wolves to save
his own skin. He didn't bother to ask me about it, but began
apologizing to the Foreign Office and anyone else who
would listen. He lost his head completely because and now
comes the real heart of the matter the incident as reported
by the press did not occur. No photog was threatened, in
fact he was told that nobody would stop him from taking a
picture at the Town Hall, but that I was inside and it might
be difficult. That is all that was said. The thing mushroomed
because without asking anyone the facts Butterworth got
scared. He had the chance to stop the editorial in the first
place, but when the editor realized Butterworth was so
dense he saw a chance to embarrass the United States and
the man running for reelection as Prime Minister. It's
funny because the PM is not particularly pro-American and
the two things don't go together! The press man at the
Embassy was also totally inadequate. Fortunately the S.S.
boys kept their heads or it would have been much worse. B.
wanted them to apologize, which would have been
ridiculous. The crux of it is that as reported nothing of the
kind happened. I can't stress that enough. Now wait 'til I get
home, and I am quite serious, I want to talk with you and
Mr. Acheson together. I hate to bother you with this but I
have never seen firsthand before a man in high position try

to put the blame on the little man who couldn't fight back, namely the S.S. boys. I get sick and tired of them and they make mistakes, but I will not sit calmly by and listen to a complete lie about a situation which was the fault of the chief of the mission.

Stockholm was a beautiful city, but that Town Hall wasn't worth the trouble it caused. We had a wonderful boat ride to Helsinki and a huge crowd cheered us off the boat. There were some Americans on the boat. Helsinki is a bright, clean-looking city. The Legation[?] is quite nice and the Cabots are very hospitable. Everything has gone fine here thanks to a capable Ambassador + a fine Press Attaché. Now I have been carrying this in my case for two days so I'd calm down even more before sending it. Goodness knows you have enough important troubles without having any from me. However, I still believe Butterworth and his attachés to be to blame for the whole thing by their pusillanimous attitude. I changed some of this letter and I'm sorry it's so messy, but I haven't the strength to copy it.

Give it to 'em on Sept. 1st and show everybody who's still on top and in control of the situation. I see you and Mother are going to Europe without me next year. I have news for you, you just try to take that whole trip without me! Please, I'd like to come.

See you next weekend.

Lots of love
Margie

? TO ?—DATE UNKNOWN, PROBABLY BETWEEN APRIL AND
JULY 1945

Sunday

Dear Daddy,

It must be quite exciting where you are. Plenty going on. Jane and I have plenty going on here but in a different way. Everybody has been so nice and there has been a party every day. We, Mother too, are going to Lake Lotawana to Major's and Mrs. Strickler's to swim and then to eat at the boat club. It's a perfect day. The sun is hot but it's cool in the shade and a nice breeze blowing.

I have a new album of Nelson Eddy records and I like them even if nobody else in the family does. Have done some singing in Church and hope to do some more.

Mamma Truman and Aunt Mary are fine and I call them every time I hear from you. They have had to have a fire it's been so cold. We had the furnace turned on.

You be careful and watch Stalin and Churchill. C. especially. Everybody over here is back of you and they're all pulling for you. Be good and if you have time send me a letter from Potsdam.

Loads of love
"Sistie"

? TO ?—DATE UNKNOWN

Dear Daddy,

Here are two songs in English!! Hope you approve.
Have been working hard.

Love,
Margie

? TO ?—DATE UNKNOWN

Dear Daddy,

Please sign your John Hancock on these 11 dollar bills
for Rosalind. Thank you. (Don't you have a single pen that
works?)

Sistie

You didn't try all of them, Dad

Bess Truman
to Margaret Truman

"When I was about six or seven years old," my father once wrote about my mother, Bess Truman, "my mother took me to Sunday school and I saw there the prettiest, sweetest little girl I'd ever seen. I was too backward even to look at her very much and I didn't speak to her for five years.

"From the fifth grade in school until my graduation from high school, we were in the same classes. If I succeeded in carrying her books to school or back home for her I had a big day."

For over a quarter of a century, from that day on which Dad first espied her until he married his first and only love, Elizabeth Virginia Wallace, known as Bess, Dad was to court my mother relentlessly, in person and by mail.

So indefatigable was he that for a time he commuted twenty miles on Saturday nights for his precious weekly dates with her. He also continued the courtship by correspondence while he was away, writing her love letters from the battlefields in France while World War I raged all around him.

Bess was slim, with fine skin and the most beautiful eyes he'd ever seen. She also had some unusual abilities for a woman in those days. She was supposed to be able to whistle through her teeth, play an admirable game of baseball, and a mean game of mumblety-peg. She was also an outstanding tennis player, and once won a shotput in a track meet. She was later to state jokingly that such a talent came in handy for training her to shake hands with a thousand people at a time.

Athletic prowess aside, though, most of all Bess Truman was—and always will be—a lady. Throughout my youth, she was determined to teach me to be the same. While I'll admit that I did not always do everything that she wanted me to do, at least I didn't get into any serious scrapes, make headlines with any scandals, or do anything ever to embarrass her or my father.

Although I loved both of my parents equally, like most young women, and as one would expect in our situation, I spent more time with my mother than father. We first became close when we started living in Washington while Dad was still a Senator.

Possibly it was my age then, or maybe she felt that I could get into less trouble in Washington than I could with my friends in Independence. But she began to relax her maternal grip. Our relationship then developed much more into one of friendship than the usual mother-daughter situation.

Even though she always managed to find time to spend with me, or write to me when we were apart, she was an incredibly busy lady as is obvious from her correspondence. In addition to the political duties, first as a judge's wife, then as a Senator's wife, then as a Vice-President's wife, and then finally, for almost eight years, as a President's wife, she was also a part-time assistant to Dad during his earlier political years.

In those days, Dad sometimes liked to jokingly refer to her as "The Boss." She didn't think it was one bit amusing and she was far more successful than I was with "Baby" in finally being able to break him of that habit.

My letter-writing relationship with Mother was as one-sided as with Dad, although it didn't seem to bother Mother that I didn't write her back. She dashed off chatty letters to me when she had a moment, and while Dad enclosed money in his envelopes, she usually referred to newsclippings that she was always sending along in hers.

Some of those articles were about me; others were about people that we both knew. Although I appreciated receiving them in those days, I now feel that I have seen enough clippings to last a lifetime and no longer even bother to keep a scrapbook.

Mother was not quite as supportive of my desire for a career as was my father, but she did discuss my singing in her letters to me. Like Dad, she also took great pride in my voice. "You just cannot know how lovely your voice was last night to Pop and me sitting here listening," she wrote me in 1947. "Pop says he don't know anything about music but that Margaret's voice sounded 'awful sweet to him.' It was more than *sweet*—so high and pure. I cannot put in words what I felt."

Part of what she felt—and didn't put into words there—was ambivalence. She felt that I had chosen a difficult career and she would have been happier had I instead chosen to go after something easier. Like getting married and settling down. While Dad realized that I would be able to do it all in my lifetime, I think Mother would have relaxed more had I chosen to do things in a different sequence.

I don't think the public ever really understood Mother. She didn't give them any help in this either. She disliked publicity and avoided giving those long in-depth interviews First Ladies sometimes give about what they are supposedly thinking, feeling and doing. Had she done so, the public might have understood her better. But Mother was not a very public person, and she tried whenever possible to keep it that way.

Her letters to me, which follow, give a picture of her that was never seen by the public. (Note too that discussions of politics are conspicuously absent in her letters, even though politically related activities took up so much of her time.) But her letters can perhaps be better understood if you first understand her a little better, which I think you can after reading this description of her, Dad, and their differences which I wrote twenty-five years ago:

> ...."They [both] get huffy. They get mad. They get their feelings hurt. They get bored. They are both stubborn as mules ... They disagree ... One disapproves of the other's language ... One likes to dance; the other one doesn't. One likes bridge; the

other likes poker. One thinks publicity is not quite
nice. The other one knows publicity is a necessity at
certain times, and insists on it. One enjoys sitting on a
bank with a fishing pole; the other turns pale with
ennui if she has to go fishing. One leans toward the
conservative in dress. The other will wear a shirt with
hibiscus printed on it if not prevented. One takes to
flying like an eagle; the other detests flying, but will
steel herself to do it if necessity demands. Both think a
fool and his money are soon parted, and that
sometimes their daughter is foolish. One thinks the
other is always trying to spoil me, and she couldn't be
more right! One can't go to bed until I get home at
night, not because she doesn't trust me implicitly, but
because she wants to hear all about it! One goes
soundly to sleep at the drop of a hat, even on election
night, and can't understand why anybody else wants
to stay up. One thinks it is a sound idea to hear a
woman out and then make up your own mind about
the matter under discussion. The other knows a man
hasn't got the sense he was born with when it comes to
taking care of himself and is always ready with the
aspirin, the needle and thread, and the advice on wet
feet and not sitting in a draft and other instructions.
One thinks there is more than one way to skin a cat, so
when he was being nagged to mow the lawn in
Independence, Missouri the other day, he decided to
do it at 11:00 A.M. Sunday morning when everybody
was passing the house on the way to church! . . . One is
an Episcopalian and the other is a Baptist and it's
always going to be that way. They both have a strong
sense of tradition and family and . . . they both like
watermelon, each other, and me."

HOT SPRINGS NATIONAL PARK, ARK. TO INDEPENDENCE, MO.
(POSTCARD)—POSTMARKED 1942 (DATE NOT CLEAR)

Dear Margie—

I hope I find that letter in the box when I go down to breakfast. Dad is out taking a walk—but not for me! If a book from the Automobile Club of Mo. comes for me, call Ellen and have Sis come by for it.

It's plenty warm! but we have a big fan in our room. Hope you had a good time last night.

Love,
Mother

My great grandmother Gates at fifteen. An Englishwoman, she went to school with Longfellow.

HOT SPRINGS NATIONAL PARK, ARK. TO INDEPENDENCE,
MO.—POSTMARKED 15 JULY 1942

Wednesday

Dear Margie—

We were mighty glad to get your grand letter yesterday morning and a good about Davis [?] bad luck out at Brown's. I have a hunch you and May won't <u>ever</u> get him back there again. Sounds to me as if May had ice cream soup instead of i.c. cone.

Dad has been through the Gov't Clinic + they found nothing wrong but advised an <u>honest-to-goodness</u> rest.

Had a note from Millie <u>with</u> some stamps—+ she said the Helfrick girl whom she runs around with married a rich Californian last week—thirty years older than she is.

It's a little cooler this morning (went to 100 yesterday)—I sat on the porch while Dad went to the hospital + it was grand out there. There are a lot of people in this big hotel. Most of them Hebraic—and most of them halfsick. Lots of children—too bad you aren't along!

Love to everybody + be good—

Mother

WASHINGTON, D.C. TO INDEPENDENCE, MO.—POSTMARKED 5
JULY 1946

> Shangri-La-on-Catoctin Mt.
>
>   Thursday

Dear Margie—

This is the most peaceful Fourth of July I have any
recollection of. Not a sound except water dripping into the
pool out in front and Chico washing dishes in the kitchen.

It is pretty chilly unless we sit right in the sun. Have a
small fire in fireplace and a few of the heaters on.

Dad went for a long walk and a swim—but not for me!
I've been reading or just sittin'.

We are going all over the place this afternoon in a
jeep—Won't we be sore tomorrow?

You would like the picture show tonight! Anna + the
King of Siam—Two Sisters from Boston tomorrow and the
Marx Bros.' A Night in Casablanca the next night. That will
be the night I go to bed early.

We get the Wash. papers before noon.

I don't know when this will be mailed. Maybe
tomorrow. I forgot my shower cap + they are going to pick
that up in the morning so evidently no more trips today.
Rigdon is here + six S.S. men—but they don't bother us. We
are staying in the main lodge but may go to the other one
before leaving.

Hope you sent that article back to Jane right
away—What did you think of it? Hope the sun is shining
there so the picnic at Latamana[?] will be a success.

>   Love to all the family
>   Mother

Irv "gets out" this week. (Sounds like he is getting out of
prison.)

INDEPENDENCE, MO. TO WASHINGTON, D.C.—POSTMARKED 8
JULY 1946

Monday

Dear Marg—

We are back in sizzling Wash. again—and wishing for
the cool breezes at S.L. [S.L. means Shangri-La-on-Catoctin
Mt.]. There are about twenty fans going on the second floor,
but even so, the "atmosphere" is warm and muggy. I had a
big fan on the floor in my room last night so was very
comfortable.

Am sorry I wasn't there to see Fred but maybe they
won't get back until I come in Aug.

Be sure to answer this invitation <u>at once</u>.

I hope everything goes alright for your luncheon. Get a
few flowers from Cairus for the centerpiece. The lunch
napkins are in the drawer in the cabinet if V. has washed
them. Check this!

Is Leola coming to do the children's ironing?

I do hope the blue chairs get there before Sat. The very
first time I can get downtown I'll look for a lamp + send it
on out.

The mail is piled up high—R. has been gone all week +
for four days it wasn't even opened.

Am sending a lovely picture of Nancy Anderson to you.
It came several days ago. Also sending 6 boxes of Kleenix
—if you still can't get any when this is about gone, let me
know.

I think Grandmother had better get pasteurized milk
for the children—some doctors think polio is carried in raw
milk. Personally, I'd rather take a chance on Perlie's raw
milk than on a dairy's pasteurized—but Chris might not be
so sold on it.

Where is The Cook + Lernon bill? The Keith bill was
in Reathel's envelope. She is sending the history you
wanted at once. It doesn't sound like "summer reading" to
me.

Louise + Pauline + William are having lunch with us today.

Write as often as you can.

Love to all
Mother

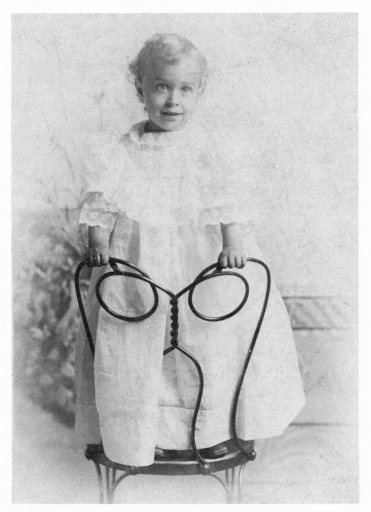

Mother at about eighteen months.

Tuesday

Dear Margie—

I am sending Vietta's check at once as she probably
wants it. Tell her Bluette said she would continue to take
care of her book + Sarver got it from B. to make the
last entry. Am also sending CK for your gas. Make some
arrangements with Mills about "charging" or pay when you
buy it. I can't send a CK every time you put in gas—please.
The first time you go to Jenkins go to the office + pay
them 68 cts. There evidently was something else on bill—+
I paid that sales slip you sent of 4.15.
It's cloudy today but mighty little cooler. Hope it's more
comfortable at home.
Is everything going alright?
Have the chairs come?

Love
Mother

WASHINGTON, D.C. TO INDEPENDENCE, MO. —POSTMARKED 10 JULY 1946

Dear Marg—

Your letter has just arrived—yes, of course use the ham—the smaller one. Is Vietta having trouble getting any meat at all? It's not very plentiful here but I <u>can</u> send some if you get really short.

Drucie is going to the hospital tonight to have her tonsils out tomorrow. I told her I would go over tomorrow afternoon to see her—Evlyn didn't come back with them last week.

Have talked to Jane two or three times. She <u>seems</u> to have made up her mind not to take that job.

The Duncans are here at the Shoreham. We are taking them "down the river" Sunday—also the Vinsons + John—+ probably the Tom Clarks, Rayburn and the Otis Blands—Hope it isn't steaming hot.

I hope everything goes off alright for your luncheon.

I'll talk to Dad about that trip to St. L. + let you know. He's gone to bed—he was so tired. The new naval aide is very nice and his family is too—two young girls 12 + 14.

They haven't found a place to live so have gone to a beach somewhere with Mrs. F.'s mother who has a cottage there.

You knew that Clark is staying on for a year as an Exec. Sec'y?—(Rosenman's place).

You had better buy yourself some stamps. I'm short, too.

Love to all
Mother

The C+S bill—please

WASHINGTON, D.C. TO INDEPENDENCE, MO. —POSTMARKED 16
JULY 1946

Tuesday

Dear Marg—

I am enclosing a paper Vietta will have to sign <u>before a
notary</u> (ask Uncle Frank) before her next paycheck goes
out—so send it back <u>very</u> soon.

It's right chilly here today—Almost <u>too</u> cool on the
porch at breakfast time.

We had a nice day on the river Sunday—was most too
warm to sit outside tho!

Drucie just called + she can talk very well today.

There are 900 USO, Red Cross, etc. workers coming to a
Garden Party today. No food tho except punch.

I am going to Olney with Mrs. L. + Jane Friday—the
long-talked-of-trip! Probably will rain!

They're building the dust + dirt cages around the
elevator "exits" today so from <u>Friday on</u> will climb the
stairs for two months.

Bess Furman is getting a story on you ready for <u>N.Y.
Times</u> sometime in August. There is also one in the making
for <u>Sat. Eve. Post</u>.

Hope you have sent that C+S bill—

Louise is back in town + called this morning.

Love to all
Mother

WASHINGTON, D.C. TO INDEPENDENCE, MO. —POSTMARKED 21
JULY 1946

Sunday
2:00 P.M.

Dear Marg—

Your S.D. airmails have just arrived + I will send Mme.
Bonnet's note tomorrow.

Am enclosing some money for you. You'd better write
to Dad about it, <u>soon</u>.

Be sure to ask Bess Furman (Armstrong) to say
nothing about seeing you. She is dependable I think + ask
her not to say she interviewed you for you would really be in
hot water. <u>You</u> can say it was just a social visit with an
out-of-towner.

I wanted to have a luncheon for Mrs. Mesta—but what
can I do if she is staying just the one day?

We had the green + glass furniture moved up on to the
porch + it looks <u>very</u> nice there. There were too many birds
roosting in the magnolias to use it comfortably there.

The elevator goes out tomorrow—sad to say—

I am going to Warrenton with L. Stewart tomorrow—to
have lunch at that Chrysler place. We've talked about it long
enough.

Drucie starts to school again on Thursday—but has
just two classes—(Milgus[?] for one).

The Novers[?] are going to Paris to cover the Peace
Conference.

They are trying to thumb a ride with J. Byrnes + Co.

The Vaughans have gone to Michigan for two weeks.
She really should stay all summer.

Annette + Irv are in NY. (Maybe I've already told you
that.) He <u>may</u> go to Georgetown next year.

Here are some clippings for you and Grandmother. Am
I sending too many? Miss Orendorf will send your
collection of funny papers tomorrow.

Love to all
Mother

WASHINGTON, D.C. TO INDEPENDENCE, MO. — POSTMARKED 31
JULY 1946

Wednesday

Dear Marg—

I want to tell you Sunday to tell Vietta to get Leola or
some one to help at dinner times while the family is all
there—There is a turkey down at the Ice Co. (ask Natalie) if
you would rather have it than the ham Sunday.

Mrs. Lingo[?] + Jane are coming over this afternoon.

Tell Natalie + May I loved their sassy card from
A.R.—Even the "Bessie" part of it.

I hope it cools off before I arrive. It's been gorgeous
here for almost a week, + now, we're spoilt.

Are C. + F. really coming right away?

I think I'll take my favorite PEO's down the river
Friday. I owe most of them luncheons and this will "square"
me.

Mrs. Mesta has been trying to get me since
yesterday—guess I'll have to talk to her today. She probably
wants to come with us. Betty is being married Sept. 7th.

Love to all
Mother

WASHINGTON, D.C. TO INDEPENDENCE, MO.—POSTMARKED 26
SEPTEMBER 1946

Thursday—

Dear Marg—

Dad enjoyed the telegram from I. Handy—

The record doesn't sound like much on this wretched
machine + I am hoping the new Capehart will be coming
soon. He is mighty anxious for copies of your other records
too—Will you be leaving yours here or taking them along
with you?

Tell Grandmother to call Cousin Helen about this letter
+ tell her I am mighty sorry I can't be there, too. Maybe Mr.
D. could take grandmother in if you can't go—you might be
able to work it out someway.

Alex called last night + sounded <u>very</u> disappointed that
you are not coming sooner. He says you <u>do</u> owe him a letter
+ to please write to him. He can't get into Columbia so is
going to work for a year + try again.

Annette was here yesterday. Irv can't get into Duke
until Feb'y so he is just going to loaf I guess. He is with
his father in Memphis right now. Mr. W. has been quite ill—

Mrs. Lingo called yesterday but they couldn't run me
down—so I didn't get to talk to her.

This floor looks grand but the first floor is still a mess
+ we are having two guests today + tomorrow (on the
porch). It is really summer weather here. We are still eating
on the porch—a little "buggy" with the lights on at night so
I think we'll move in tonight.

I sent your clothes yesterday, all except the blue skirt.
It had several moth holes so Julia took it to the textile place
+ it will be rushed thru + I'll send it in about a week.
Everything else appeared to be alright. Carter also put some
Kleenex in—give grandmother some.

Mrs. Dodson is waiting for me to call her so I guess the
Chrysler will be on its way east pretty soon.

Am plenty busy and my book is really full—don't know when I can even do any shopping.

Write me soon—

Love to all
Mother—

You can exchange these airmail stamps after Oct. 1 for 5's

Mother and Uncle Frank at a young age. Look at those curls!

WASHINGTON, D.C. TO INDEPENDENCE, MO.—POSTMARKED 2
OCTOBER 1946

Tuesday

Dear Margie—

Carter sent your blue skirt today + I hope it goes
through in a hurry for I'm sure you could use it right now.
It is still cool here but a little warmer than yesterday. They
did a grand job on it.

Louise was here this morning and brought two black
dinner dresses from Bergdorf's. One of them I think I'll
keep. Am going up there next week to look at some
things—be there Mon. + Tues. only. Going to see Ethel
Merman Mon. night.

Did you get a hat to wear with your new suit? Aunt
Natalie said she was going in with you to look for one. Tell
her + Beufy I'll write them soon. Surely enjoyed their
letters. Had one from Chris today, too. They surely are
having a siege of colds.

This clipping is from the noon news.

You might put in your idle moments writing a book!

Do you want any other clothes? Guess there isn't much
left here except formals—

Write when you can.

Love to all
Mother—

WASHINGTON, D.C. TO INDEPENDENCE, MO.—POSTMARKED 3
OCTOBER 1946

Thursday

Dear Marg—

Was glad to hear from you this morning.

I think you + Aunt Nat did a good job of shopping and I
am glad you got all of those things. You may remember that
I suggested that those particular shoes needed replacing
months ago!

I don't quite know what about the picture for Gaby. Do
you want it sent to you first so you can "inscribe" it? Do you
want one that Hessler made a year or so ago or one that was
made last spring here in the house? I'll send as soon as
you let me know. The French Dictionary goes out today.
Mrs. V.'s note has already gone.

Did I send Lady Berendson's[?] card to you? I think a
note telling her you liked being asked to her tea etc. We sent
flowers with your card yesterday. I can't remember
whether I sent you the card or not. The tea was for the
Chamber Music Guild in case I didn't send it.

I hope the gray hat matched your suit—+ you could
wear both of them today to Shawsie's luncheon. Am glad
you wrote to Mrs. Park. That's more than I have done but
dad sent a wire in both of our names. I had already wired
Sands about flowers but thanks for thinking of it.

Dad told me he sent you some money a day or two ago.

He says the appraisement is OK. The retail price is
1,200—but we wouldn't have to buy it on the retail market
to replace it.

Had a note from Chris saying she couldn't get any oleo
so I am sending her some today to tide her over. It's hard to
get here, too.

The U.S.O.—3rd Anniversary party is tonight—8:10—It
will be plenty tiresome. Guess Mrs. L. + Jane will be there

Mrs. Davis' (at Jill's) husband died just two days after
Barbara was married. Had a stroke.

Marguerite did my hair. She was very anxious to know how your permanent had turned out. Her sister Betty is back—which gives us three chances at a good operator.

> Love to everybody—
> Mother

Frank Gates Wallace, age four years and two months.

WASHINGTON, D.C. TO INDEPENDENCE, MO. — POSTMARKED
9 OCTOBER 1946

Wednesday

Pi Phi's pledged 15 or 16

Dear Marg—

We were glad to have your letter yesterday—but don't stay up until one o'clock just to write to us!

Am glad you had such a nice time on Sunday—and had a chance to see the country. Very few of the leaves here in town have turned but I went to Olney with Mrs. L. + Jane yesterday and the trees were gorgeous north of here.

Mrs. L. says to tell you that you have a date with her the day you get here! (or words to that effect.)

Pye had a luncheon for Mrs. Foskett today—just like all the others he has had parties for. Much good too—+ a beautiful ice-cream cake. It beats Baked Alaska all to pieces.

Practically every one there asked when you were coming. I called Mrs. M. fairly early Sunday morning but Vic had already called her. He started in telling her what you were doing etc. + she told him as long as he had reversed the call he could wait and tell her about it when he got home. Sounds familiar doesn't it?

Vivian + Ralph had breakfast with us this morning.

Am glad you went out to see Adelaide.

We have everything under control about Gaby's picture. That was the only Hessler picture here. I'll order a few of those—they are so much better than the new ones.

I'm sending some clippings. If I'm sending too many say so. Put these in that envelope in left-hand drawer that says "clpgs to go to Wash."

Mr. Dodson got here safely with the car but picked up a nail.

Tell Grandmother I can't get <u>any</u> paper dolls of <u>any</u> description. If there is anything I can get in place of them let me know. Sent the shirt to her Tues. Also sent her heavy coat etc. today by express.

It has cooled off considerably + is very cloudy. This has been a hectic week—every day with about four appts.

The Strauss concert was really lovely. Wish they would put on more like it.

How's your meat supply holding out? We are having an awful lot of fish—guess you are glad you are not here!

The Dr. says he will send the diet + "pills" right away. Today is his birthday.

Have I told you Louise is sailing on the <u>America</u> on the 17th?

You had better send her a small going-away gift right soon.

Tell Grandmother I'll write her soon.

Love
Mother—
Kleenex gone—

WASHINGTON, D.C. TO INDEPENDENCE, MO. —

Sunday

Dear Margie—

We have just finished lunch (after talking to you). I thought I had better get these checks off to you so Leola wouldn't be out-of-luck on Thursday.

Also I forgot to tell you to have Chasnoff's[?] send your fur coat so you will have it <u>here</u> when you get here + I'll have R. get your jacket from Garfinckel's so it will be ready to take with you—Yes, put your light blue long dress in the bag—does it need cleaning + is that rip in the hem fixed?

What kind of a brown hat did you get? You are going to need some sort of a gay silly little one for afternoons, too—but wait until you get here. How do you like your new suit by this time?

If Mme. Bonnet + Roberta T. go to Paris in March—I imagine you will be with them—if you are not otherwise tied up—

Saw Marvin at the wedding but not to talk to. Jane + Drucie looked cute—Jane has a new pink feather hat! I don't know whether she had on black or brown with it. Drucie had a so-called hat of three short ostrich tips over one ear. She has a new short fur jacket—very good-looking. John is sick—he + Evlyn were here to dinner last night (also JK + Bee) + he had to leave before he'd ever had dinner—had a hard[?] chill going home + some fever later—but is better today. Wish you were going to N.Y. with me tomorrow.

Hope Dan is better.

Love
Mother

[Letter included one newspaper clipping entitled "Arrives for 'Met' Debut"—next to that Bess Truman had written "Who's next?" Underneath photo it reads: "Renée Mazella, French operatic soprano, is greeted by Edward Johnson, President of the Metropolitan Opera Association. Renée's South American season, just completed, was trés triumphant, and she'll make her debut with the 'Met' this season."]

WASHINGTON, D.C. TO INDEPENDENCE, MO. — POSTMARKED 24
OCTOBER 1946

Thursday

Dear Marg—

Well, we are back in harness after a hectic yesterday.

I had promised Mrs. Burton weeks ago I would come to
her Com. chest luncheon so had to go—+ had to leave before
Elsa Maxwell's talk in order to catch the plane! at 2:30. We
got to N.Y. at 3:40 + were whisked to the U.N. Bldg. +
rushed into a reception room where Sie[?] + somebody else
"greeted" us—then to auditorium where Spaak made a
speech—in French—+ then Dad's speech. Then about 75
motor police took us to the Waldorf where I had to hurry +
dress for the reception. I wore the long-sleeved dress with
gold comb. in front that I had last winter + Louise loaned
me her black velvet grape hat! We shook hands with 835
(according to H. Vaughan) + then rushed to dress to make
the train at 8:25. The Byrneses came home with us so we
had to be polite + sit up + talk all the way home when I had
planned a good nap. Kind of sleepy this morning.

Louise has no idea when she will get off. John couldn't
get her on the [Queen] Elizabeth. She is plenty disgusted.

They are painting the basement corridor + putting in
another door + partition just east of the old map room. It
will cut off a lot of draft in cold weather and make a good
"break" down there. The new carpets will be dark green, the
walls light green + some new benches + consoles are due
any day. Have made a beautiful room out of the old billiard
room + hung some of the "gal's" pictures in there.

The elevator is still not working perfectly—but is very
snappy looking + really gets up + goes.

Your new fur coat has not come. Have you told them?
The evening jacket is here in the cedar room + R. is getting
both of our coats today from [?].

These clippings are really honies [sic]. [Five clippings
on Margaret Truman's singing are in letter—from gossip
columns.]

Am sending Drucie a large bunch of mums tonight at Lisner—all three names on card. I want to go tonight or tomorrow. Evlyn said Sparkie was most enthusiastic last night. Evlyn has had some more teeth out + according to Dr. G. she is in a bad way.

We may all four go to Shangri-La for the weekend.

Love to all
Mother

Lucy Moffett is having a luncheon at CC Club tomorrow for me.

Vietta Garr, who was always
there when we needed her.

WASHINGTON, D.C. TO INDEPENDENCE, MO. — POSTMARKED
28 OCTOBER 1946

Monday—

Dear Marg—

Here we are back in harness after a nice weekend. The weather was perfect and every one had a nice time I think.

The trees were gorgeous on the whole trip. Dad + I stayed over in the new guest house + it is very comfortable except for the beds—they are terrible. The food was good + Chico is still in charge.

Drucie really did a wonderful job in her play. I surely wish you could have seen it.

Rose had a letter from Mrs. Litson saying many nice things about you. The new radio hasn't come but I <u>hope</u> it will be here by the sixth.

Louise <u>expects</u> to sail the last of this week.

Will be seeing you soon!

Love
Mother

WASHINGTON, D.C. TO NEW YORK CITY — POSTMARKED
12 NOVEMBER 1946

Monday night

Dear Babe—

Just a line or two. Don't imagine you have time to read
more than that anyway.

It is now eight thirty o'clock so I am sure you are
not far from the Met. Am glad I have a good picture of it in
my mind. I wish the opera was being broadcast, as last year.

It's raining tonight + kind of dismal. Dad is having a
"party" in the study. There's no doubt but what George Allen
is "among those present."

If you have time, send a card to Roberta Vinson. I do
hope Mme. Bonnet got you. She was most anxious to. Even
called us herself!

Mrs. Jim Trimble is going to help us choose + get some
new drapes for the study. Can't stand those strings any
longer. She is in touch with several N.Y. shops. Sloane's
materials are no good. John sent me a Chinese horse—it
will have to go in your Cabinet. (Jade.)

Ordered a "flower" hat today for one of these dismal
teas. Give my best to [?] + May.

Lots of love
Mother

WASHINGTON, D.C. TO NEW YORK CITY—POSTMARKED
19 NOVEMBER 1946

Dear Marg—

I am sending your grandmother T. some gloves for her birthday from you.

I would suggest that a postcard to the family in Independence + Grandmother might be in order. They are a bit peeved that they have had not a word from you (or were when I heard last). And it does seem to me, too, that you might have time to send a card.

This is a busy week. Had a letter from Dad this morning + he is <u>really</u> enjoying the Florida sunshine.

Love
Mother

WASHINGTON, D.C. TO NEW YORK CITY—POSTMARKED
21 NOVEMBER 1946

Dear Marg—

Mrs. Krug asked me yesterday if someday when you are here you would dedicate the new music room just finished at Walter Reed. It's in connection with their music-therapy project. Told her I would just have to ask you.

Hope N.Y. is as warm + sunshiny as Wash. is today.

Two large teas today—Wish you were here to stand in line!

Jane is coming to the Diplomatic dinner Tues. Asked Drucie but she had an engagement. We are long on men! Drucie has been to all the shows with "Sparkie"!

The New Moon production by Columbia Light Opera Co. was splendid. The Snyders, Lingos[?] + I went.

Didn't intend to write a letter when I started.

Love
Mother

WASHINGTON, D.C. TO INDEPENDENCE, MO. — POSTMARKED
1946 (DATE NOT CLEAR)

Monday morning

Dear Marg—

Your cold wave caught up with us last night + it is
much cooler this A.M.

Your Special came late yesterday afternoon and we
both enjoyed it.

Mr. Dodson will probably be there sometime this week
for the car. Will you ask Mr. Dorsey if he will please have
Mills wash it + clean inside thoroughly but not change
grease etc. as it hasn't been 100 miles since it was done in
June. I told Mrs. D. that—Anyway Mr. Dodson can do as he
pleases about that. Everything is arranged + I think Mr.
Nicholson wrote some one about plates for him.

It was nice talking to you and grandmother yesterday.
We spent the day here in the house. May go to Shangri-La
after the Dem. tea next Sat.

Miss [Mrs.] McLaughlin telephoned about the
"provisional" dinner next Friday. I told her that you had
been delayed in returning etc.—something you couldn't
help + she said you could talk to Mrs. Willett when you got
here about your work. It's too bad you weren't here to do it
as they are getting all of it into three weeks!

Hope you get a nice-looking hat for Thursday—you
probably would have better luck at Harz[?] or Woolfs than
at Rachel's.

I haven't found a thing so far—May go this afternoon
again as I need a hat this week—

Love to all
Mother

I think we get the elevator today. That's really big
news.

WASHINGTON, D.C. TO NEW YORK CITY — POSTMARKED
4 FEBRUARY 1947

Tuesday A.M.

Dear Marg—

We were mighty glad to get your note yesterday.

Mrs. Sharpe sent you a heterogenous (don't check the spelling) collection of mats + napkins yesterday she said. If they are <u>too</u> bad, I'll go downtown + get you a few—in case of guests?—

Everyone on the place is getting ready for the Alexanders today. They arrive at four for tea—then dinner + the lengthy reception. Help! (or leave off the "p" + add another "l").

It's very cloudy + misting + feels like snow.

We (Mr. West + I) decided this morning to <u>do</u> something about the Monroe room—at least get some slips for those horrible striped chairs + new drapes—

Did you hear Walter Winchell broadcast the offer to you from that Hollywood picture company? Evidently the company turned it loose for advertising.

Jane came over for a little while yesterday. I think she is already very "homesick" for you. Hope you found the things <u>alright</u>. Love to Mrs. S.

Much love from
Mother + Dad

WASHINGTON, D.C. TO NEW YORK CITY—POSTMARKED
5 FEBRUARY 1947

Thelma is having lunch   Wednesday A.M.
with us today!!!

Margie, dear—

I am sending a box of brownies that Mr. Dan Nibs
brought dad from a friend of his in Baltimore—I ate one +
they are really delicious (even beat Pete's) and your black
bag—It is so much nicer looking than that satin one of
mine.

The Alexanders are most attractive + we had a really
nice small dinner for them in the family dining room—The
Nimitzes were here + raving about you. The Admiral said
he did not intend to miss your debut!

The reception of course was horrible—1,341—+ my
arm is a wreck this A.M.

Janet Vaughan is in a serious condition with blood
poisoning in her hand. In fact Dr. G. said if he had seen her
48 hours later he couldn't have done a thing for her—+ if
he hadn't had penicillin there would have been no chance
for her when he did see her. Mrs. V. is terribly worried today
as her arm is swollen this morning. They brought her right
back from W + M, fortunately.

Cute little Marian Cummings was elected Pres. of Pi
Phi—

The Lady-in-Waiting to Lady Alexander was a lovely
nineteen-year-old niece of hers. I wish you could have been
here.

Love to both of you
Mother

WASHINGTON, D.C. TO NEW YORK CITY—POSTMARKED 6
FEBRUARY 1947

Dear Marg—

Helen Sioussat (pronounced Sousa) called yesterday +
wanted your address to send you an invitation of some sort.

She is the radio girl who was here in Jan'y '46
with the actors etc. at lunch + was here to call just before
Christmas this year. She is a very nice person + apparently
has nothing to "sell"—but <u>may</u> be of much help to you later
on—as she has already offered to do anything she can for
you. As far as I can figure, she has a <u>real</u> job in radio—She
also wrote that book <u>Mikes Don't Bite</u>—Maybe you
remember all this but I wanted to be sure.

Love,
Mother

Do you need any money?

WASHINGTON, D.C. TO NEW YORK CITY—POSTMARKED 8
FEBRUARY 1947

Sat. A.M.

Dear Margie—

Mrs. V. just called + said they enjoyed so much seeing
both of you last night. Also told me that you missed hearing
Munsel—+ that the soprano + tenor each missed a note—

Dad had a stag dinner for Mr. Householder from
Phoenix—a member of his old Battery. I guess they told
some tall war stories. One of his sons was shot down over
Germany + someone saw him bailing out + that was the
last they ever heard of him.

If you have a chance to get valentines don't forget the
family + grandmother.

Here's a Flagstad (Kirsten) item you'll be interested in.
Also part of John Friant's letter.

These two weeks are really going to be a handshaking
two weeks—conservative estimate 4,100—I'll be plenty glad
when Feb'y 19 arrives!

I hear M.S. told Maj. to come on + bring his checkbook.
Do you need any money? Don't let her pay anything for you.

Just heard that Jimmie Davidson's mother died
yesterday—Better write him + I will, too—

Love—
Mother

WASHINGTON, D.C. TO NEW YORK CITY (POSTCARD)—
POSTMARKED 24 FEBRUARY 1947

Shawsie's package was in the mail before you got to N.Y.

Be sure to write to your grandmother T. soon if you haven't already done it.

Love,
Bess T.

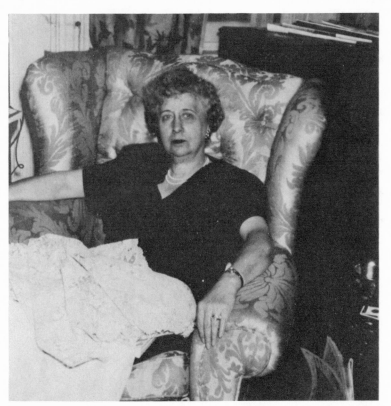

My favorite among my photographs of Mother. In the library of Blair House, 1949.

WASHINGTON, D.C. TO NEW YORK CITY—POSTMARKED 25
FEBRUARY 1947

Tuesday A.M.

Dear Margie—

Mrs. Clifford called yesterday + gave me this schedule
for St. L. Operas. I'm sending it just as I put it down.

Louise called yesterday A.M. + said she had enjoyed
talking to you and Marvin called last night. I didn't tell him
I had talked to you.

I hope Maj. got in safely + that all of you are having a
good time.

Would you like to have that Cadwallader scarf of mine
that has the bright red squares on it to wear with your new
suit? I'll send it with the suit if you want it. That suit needs
something other than a white blouse.

The New Yorkers + Vinsons + Snyders are coming to
lunch today—Imagine we'll have a gay time.

We heard Tagliavini last night—He is really
something.

Am getting all the birthday presents off today. I got two
very good-looking handkerchiefs for you to send Frankie +
a silk slip for Marian.

Love
Mother—

INDEPENDENCE, MO. TO WASHINGTON, D.C. — POSTMARKED 17
MARCH 1947

Independence
Monday morning

Dearest Marg—

    You just cannot know how lovely your voice was last
night to Pop and me sitting here listening. Pop says he don't
know anything about music but that Margaret's voice
sounded "awful sweet to him." It was more than sweet—so
high and pure. I cannot put in words what I felt. I told Aunt
Cam to write a poem about it. She said she would if the
words would come. You will be getting worlds of
congratulations but this is just love from

Mom

WASHINGTON, D.C. TO NEW YORK CITY—POSTMARKED 30
APRIL 1947

Tues. 10:00 A.M.

Dear Marg—

I had a most delightful weekend but it was much too
short.

We had a nice trip home but I don't want to <u>drive</u> again
right away. The traffic outside of N.Y. was terrific.

The whole household is busily getting ready for El
Presidente this A.M. Will be happy when Thursday comes +
all this is behind us.

I forgot to give you that dollar for Caroline (maid). I
found it still in my pocket when I got home.

Be sure to check when you pay the next bill—that that
check for 50.25 is taken off. You made a slight mistake in
your supper bill. I was sure there was something wrong
with your figure. The asparagus itself was 10.—chicken etc.
16.00—etc. $7. But it was very nice + nicely served so it was
worth it.

Roberta called this A.M. and said the Duchess said she
would like for you + R. to have lunch or tea (forgotten
which) on 6-7-or 8 of May. I told R. I would tell you.

The Senate Women's luncheon today was something!
The nicest one they have ever had they said—+ certainly
the best one I remember.

Your laundry, shoes + print dress are ready to go up
tomorrow. Mr. Nicholson said he would see they got off +
call Mr. D. about them.

Hope you are fine.

The Marines + The Navy are <u>all</u> in the front yard
waiting for Alemán—+ the sun is shining + the flowers are
beautiful.

Lots of love
Mother

P.S. Will see Santleman today.
P.P.S. Beufy + Dan are surely coming on 11th + maybe the
others.

WASHINGTON, D.C. TO NEW YORK CITY — POSTMARKED 30
APRIL 1947

Tues. 4:00 P.M.

Dear Marg—

The enclosed shows why Lindsay cannot go on your
trip with you. It would take a Presidential order which
under the circumstances is not possible. Besides,
Santleman told dad that Mr. L. is in no <u>physical condition</u> to
do it. Am sorry to have to tell you this because I know you
wanted him badly.

The Mexican President is quite attractive + the small
tea went off alright + Dad said the big dinner last night was
a great success. Monteros was delighted with your picture.

Mme. Bonnet is ill—someone said pneumonia—I am
sending flowers to her today—enclosing your card
too—You had better send her a brief note <u>at once</u>.

Lots of love
Mother—

WASHINGTON, D.C. TO INDEPENDENCE, MO. — POSTMARKED 7
AUGUST 1947

Wednesday

Dear Marg—

I thought maybe you might enjoy Jane's letter if you
have time to read it. It <u>is</u> perfectly legible for once. Guess
they will be in today.

It was nice talking to both of you last night.

I hope you won't have too large a job, packing in all
that heat. Today is going to be a stinger here too.

Pye is having one of his "parties" today—much heavy
food in that hot room!

Tomorrow I am going to Olney with Mrs. Donegly +
one or two others.

Ben + Orine + the young niece are coming to tea at five
today. We'll certainly have to have something <u>cold</u> to drink.

Tell Natalie + May I surely enjoyed their letters
yesterday + will write soon.

Please tell Vietta to gather up the things (on a separate
sheet) + get a box out of the attic + ship to me. I'll need
most of them in Rio.

The Magnavox people have just given dad a radio etc.
like the one they bought for Pres. Alemán. It is being put in
the study but he says if you like it better than the Capehart
it can go into your room.

Julia + Bluetto say they are having the best time all by
themselves on 3rd floor. The grouchy Lillian + Wilma are
taking their vacations. Tell V. she ought to be here to enjoy
it with them.

The Air Force Band is giving us a concert on the lawn
tomorrow night.

Am glad Dorsey is going to be with you in Calif. How did
you "work" it?

Love to all
Mother

Thurs A.M.

Dear Marg—

Thought you might be interested in these clippings.

We are going to Shangri-La tomorrow to stay until
Mon. morning but I have told Julia about the dresses +
shoes + R. has gone down to get your coat + Mr. Rowley
says he will see that it gets on a plane and will let Nick
know which one.

This telegram just arrived—I don't know how you will
get his address—

This note is from Cousin Aline Halsey + I thought
Grandmother might like to see it—

It's getting warmish this A.M. I surely am glad it has
cooled off out there.

Mrs. Mesta just called from N. + was all steamed up
about going to L.A. but I think I persuaded her to wait for
Pittsburgh. She wants Dad + me to come up for a weekend
but you know darn well he's not going—

Jane + her mother have gone to Tyro until Aug. 15.

Annette + Irv are in Cleveland for two months for the
races there. Irv has two horses now and is training others.
Jeannette says this business is just to last one year. Guess
that's as long as Papa will back him. They are going to
Florida for the winter.

I am pretty sure the big plane will be out there to bring
you back whether we come or not. John + H.V. say it's out
of this world for traveling.

The whole first floor is in the most awful mess you
have ever seen. Painting the East room + hall + starting on
State Dining room today. The Red room will soon have a
new crystal chandelier + all the new drapes are ready to go
up as soon as the painting is finished. Your room is
absolutely ok + we will get new curtains for your bathroom.
What color do you want? They are so faded there is no color
left.

How about my dress at Mrs. L.'s? I need it. Let me know
ahead of time when you need some more money for
expenses around there.

Mrs. Helm was in for a little while yesterday.
Are you taking Mr. Nolan + Mrs. Gossard with you?
Let me definitely know when you are leaving.

Love to all
Mother

Drucie lands on 14th

WASHINGTON, D.C. TO BEVERLY HILLS, CALIF.—POSTMARKED
19 AUGUST 1947

Monday 5:00 P.M.

Dear Marg—

Have just heard by way of <u>radio</u> + ticker that you have
arrived! Hope you had a <u>really</u> comfortable trip.

I know you will be interested in this clipping—Drucie
was here yesterday—+ was somewhat "put out" as she had
told Jocelyn on Sat. she would have to wait until today to
tell her definitely whether she could do it or not—+
<u>yesterday</u> these notices were in all the Sun. papers! It's very
evident she is simply having a <u>publicity</u> wedding. [The
notice being referred to here is of the announcement of the
marriage of Jocelyn Freer to Norman C. Keith and the
announcement of Drucie Snyder as maid of honor.] I
understand Jane to say those other two girls are not
especially good friends of hers either. D. says she will go on
+ do it as it would stir up too much conversation if she
refuses. She even called Marian Cummings + asked for D.'s
dress size before D. ever came home! Well that's enough for
her. But I've decided she's too big a mess to send an
engagement present + wedding too—I am so thankful you
had a real excuse for refusing. It's disgusting.

It's a bit cooler today + I've been downtown—needed
hose + chafese for the Rio trip.

Mr. Braverman came with the Snyders yesterday.

Jim + Mary Calvert + Mrs. L. Had a dip in the pool this
morning. I am going to Lingos to lunch tomorrow. Will
probably get more "low-down".

Am writing this on my lap listening to the radio.

I do hope <u>everything</u> works out as you want it
to—especially next week—
John says the Rio trip is really something—

Lots of love—
Mother

Am so glad Maj. is there with you. Sorry you had to bother
with my clothes—Nick came today. Don't bring that
perfume. I'll get it when I go home in Sept. I think I'll go
right after the Rio trip—dad, too.

This writing looks as if I'm drunk but it's too early in
the day! My best to the Stricklers.

B.W.T.

WASHINGTON, D.C. TO INDEPENDENCE, MO. — POSTMARKED
28 OCTOBER 1947

Tuesday

Dear Marg—

Please wire me when you expect to arrive in Ft. Worth
+ how long you will be there so John can wire Mr. Carter.
Also I do not think these various rooms + apts. are to be
donated. If the suite at the club is Mr. Carter's that may be
donated—but see that there is no misunderstanding on
Mrs. S.'s part about that.

It seems to me that practically everyone I've talked to
lately is on the trail of tickets to Const. Hall on the 22nd.

Mary + Polly got off yesterday—by way of
Williamsburg—Miss J. is probably having a spell as she
wrote Polly she wanted to go home Wed.

The tail end of your big rain caught up with us this
morning + we got a brief shower—the first in thirty days.

I hope the boxes I've sent got there alright. Did your
watch come?

I sent the gift to Gloria yesterday. It looked fine. I
unwrapped it to check on the initials.

Send that wire!

Love,
Mother

Just talked to Annette. She + Irv are going to Tampa for the
winter.
Have you thanked Mr. H. for the coffee?

WASHINGTON, D.C. TO INDEPENDENCE, MO. — POSTMARKED
31 OCTOBER 1947

Dear Marg—

Here are the stamps you asked for—be sure you use them! If even on postcards.

Your schedule seems fairly stiff to me but I guess you know best.

Lieman + K. came over yesterday morning and stayed about an hour. I couldn't have them to lunch or dinner as I was going to the Carlton to lunch + we had a family dinner for H. Vaughan's mother last night—Just the V.'s + the Snyders.

Mr. Blalock of Texas is making arrangements at the Capitol for you. He told dad that <u>no</u> hotel in the South would refuse Vietta as long as she is your maid.

The Dem. Com. is presenting Mrs. McNamara's portrait of dad to me today—If they get through on time I am going out to Jeannette's to lunch. She has a friend from Hawaii in town.

Perle will be in town today + I will call her tonight + relay your messages.

Drucie is coming over to stay with us several days while Evlyn + John go on a brief "speaking tour."

They have had a big run on tickets for Dec. 22ⁿᵈ. Not a box left today. Mr. Hayes sent me 3 boxes! but I will keep only two. Had a nice note from him.

Shall probably talk to you before you get this.

Lots of love and good luck—
Mother

Friday noon

Portrait presented! + I'm off to lunch. Mrs. MH[?] came down for it.

KANSAS CITY, MO. TO NEW YORK CITY — POSTMARKED
22 OCTOBER 1954

Thursday

Dear Marg—

Thanks loads for Pat's new book. It should be good, and thanks, too, for the clpgs. One of them we had not seen, and I have put all of them away in the clipping file so if you ever want my fairly recent ones they will be easy to find.

Dad moved back upstairs this morning while I was getting breakfast. Guess he wanted to avoid any argument!

Mr. Rayburn is due at three + no telling how many others. I am getting out all the liquor glasses in the place—also all the liquor.

Love
Mother

Monday 28th A.M.
before breakfast

Dear Marg and Clifton—

It was wonderful to talk to both of you Sat. evening. The laryngitis was practically worth it—of course as long as you <u>had</u> to have it!

Today, Shirley and I are going shopping—but I am very sure I shall come home with a lot of things I won't want at all, when I get there. Mr. Haight's buyer is going with us, but if he is selecting things in Shirley's bracket I shall be out on a limb.

The Consul General and his wife Service[?] are very nice + gave us a blow-by-blow trip around Florence yesterday. We had lunch at a perfectly fabulous villa belonging to a Mr. Berenson—who is the greatest living authority on Renaissance Art and of course his place is filled with priceless things.

Tomorrow we go to Venice by train. The drive here from Rome was wonderful—as you know. I would like to go back to peaceful Assisi and stay a long time.

We have a very handsome suite here at the Excelsior and more service than we can use.

Hope your throat is loads better by this time. Also hope you won't have to go to Calif. on July 3rd.

Much love to both of you.
Devotedly
Mother

Pls check on reservation at Carlyle for July 3–7.

PARIS, FRANCE TO NEW YORK CITY—POSTMARKED ?

Sorry of course about yours and Clifton's decision but I must confess not too surprised. Hope to find that letter in Rome tomorrow. We had a long drive around Paris yesterday + Stanley and I <u>walked</u> thru the Luxembourg Gardens. Dad's ankle greatly improved. Lunching today at Dutch Embassy. That itinerary was given to you just on purpose.

> Love to both of you.
> BWT

Dear Marg and Clifton—

This is my <u>first</u> note aboard. We are so far having an
extremely smooth trip. Even pop can't complain.

This boat is everything you said it is. The food is <u>really</u>
good but as yet I have restrained myself along that line.

Sen. Benton had lunch with us today and with some
bit-off-color stories entertained? most of the private dining
room.

Shirley and Stanley are fine traveling companions—
doing far more than necessary to make our trip pleasant.

Having cocktails with the Capt. tonight—refused
others. Pop says he is not going to start <u>that</u>. (He can get his
own!!)

(Will add to this if anything of interest).

Monday A.M.

Thank you <u>very</u> much for the "timely" wire yesterday.
It was good of you to think of it.

The Norman Armours are aboard right next to us. They
are embarrassingly loud in their praise of you, Marg. They
asked us for cocktails last night + then they had dinner
with us—and we had a gay evening. Dad is thoroughly
enjoying the trip since it has been very smooth most of the
time—I am trying to get a few notes written—I don't know
<u>when</u> I'll get all these flowers etc. thanked for—

We had a small cocktail party here in our quarters
yesterday at noon (horrible thought) for some people we
had to see because <u>someone</u> had asked us to.

Stanley and I had a hot game of Ping-Pong yesterday.
No need to say anything further about <u>that</u>.

It's rolling a bit this morning but Dad is not
complaining as yet.

He is enjoying a massage right now—and has already
made eleven o'clock appointments for every morning on
return trip.

Haven't seen much of Mrs. S.—

Both of you take care of yourselves and write!!

Lots of love
Mother

Thursday, June 14th

Dear Marg and Clifton—

Am waiting for breakfast so can get at least a short
note off to you.

I am afraid, C., I have not told you we enjoyed your good
letter and shall be <u>very glad</u> to take care of your clothes on
the <u>U</u>.S.

We had dinner with the Spaaks last night—very fancy
but on the whole agreeable. The Foreign Minister + M.
Gutt[?] wanted to be remembered to you.

We are leaving shortly for the audience with the King,
which leaves me cold.

Two weeks from today we shall be on the ship headed
home. Speed the day! These one-night stands are not much
fun and as for packing and unpacking!—I'm thru for a long
time to come.

Brussels is a lot more interesting than I expected to
find it—

Much love
Mother

THE HAGUE, HOLLAND TO NEW YORK CITY (POSTCARD)—
POSTMARKED JUNE 1956 (DATE NOT CLEAR)

No mail at The Hague! so don't say another word about <u>me</u>
not writing. More rain—have almost forgotten what the
sun looks like.

> Love to you both
> BWT

THE HAGUE, HOLLAND TO NEW YORK CITY

Saturday
June 16, 1956

Dear Marg and Clifton—

We are taking off very soon for Amsterdam and a trip thru the canals + lunch aboard something—I don't know what—as someone besides Ambassador Matthews has the Embassy boat.

I've been such an extra flutterbrain on this trip—I can't remember whether I have told you to please ask Mr. Levens[?] to exchange our reservations from the 7th to the 5th. You have our tickets.

We had lunch at the beach hotel (spelling eludes me) yesterday with the P.M. and there were some very agreeable people there speaking English no less. Tonight, the Amb.'s dinner + tomorrow lunch with the Queen + then to England. If we live thru those ten days in England, I'm convinced we shall live forever. I put my large foot down on a dinner tonight with Churchill's physician in the country and I think when S. found out they were not invited he wasn't so hell-bent on <u>us</u> going.

So far, we are all very amiably inclined towards one another—but who knows?

Several people asked about you at the lunch—For. Min. Lewis + Min. Beyen + his wife. The Luns are friends of Louise's.

Must get my bonnet on. S. is a fiend for getting <u>everyone else</u> ready on time.

Lots of love—
Mother

LONDON, ENGLAND TO NEW YORK CITY (POSTCARD)—
POSTMARKED 23 JUNE 1956

We are still having a busy and happy time. We are rapidly
winding up our trip. Going to the tower today by launch.
The Archbishop of Canterbury asked to be remembered to
you.

Love to both of you—
B.W.T.

LONDON, ENGLAND TO NEW YORK CITY (POSTCARD)—
POSTMARKED 25 JUNE 1956

Monday

We are starting our last whirl of gayety and then to the
boat for HOME. Will be glad among other things to get a
good hairdo again.

Love to you both
Mother

Grandmother Wallace to Margaret Truman

My grandmother Wallace. I grew up in her house, which we all
loved.

FINALLY, also included in this collection of family correspondence are miscellaneous letters from lesser-known members of our family (mostly from Aunt Mary and Grandmother Wallace) which will round out the portrait of our close-knit family.

When I was young, and living in Independence, almost all of my immediate relatives lived nearby: Uncle Frank Wallace, Aunt Natalie, Uncle George Wallace and Aunt May were all just a stone's throw from our house. My mother's youngest brother, Fred, was unmarried then and still lived in our home. My Uncle Vivian Truman, Aunt Louella, and their family lived on a nearby farm, and my Aunt Mary Truman, along with Grandmother Martha Ellen Truman, lived a few miles away in Grandview, Missouri.

The Wallace side of the family (Mother's) which originally came from Kentucky, produced the only other politician in the immediate family. My grandfather, David Willock Wallace, was Assistant Docket Clerk of the Missouri State Senate by the age of fourteen, and later held a number of other public offices, including that of County Treasurer.

He died when my mother was young, and his widow, Grandmother Wallace (Mrs. David Willock Wallace) brought her daughter (Bess) and her three sons up in Independence in the same house which my great-grandfather had built. Mother was raised and still lives in this same house where I was later to be brought up, the house on North Delaware Street in Independence, Missouri.

Grandmother Wallace lived in that house until her death, and we had the type of loose relationship that children often have when they're brought up in the same homes with their grandmothers.

Grandmother and I also shared the same love of music, for she had once been educated at the Cincinnati

Conservatory of Music. Unlike me, however, Grandmother despised anything to do with the stage, and she
had the antiquated notion that no real lady would ever
associate herself with anything so vulgar.

She had acquired her musical training solely as a polite art for a lady, and she believed that polite ladies did not
display their talents in public. Even after I chose a singing
career, and was already singing publicly on the stage,
Grandmother would frequently let me know in no uncer-
tain terms exactly what she thought of that!

I forgave her for this, perhaps because she had so
much to forgive me for. I had been an extremely active
child, and was always tearing around her (our) house on
my little tricycle. It must have been difficult for her to
watch a young child knocking over her precious antique
possessions. Still, she kept her tongue, and I tried to do the
same when she expressed her outdated opinions.

My father, however, was not quite as tolerant of his
opinionated mother-in-law. Perhaps he and Grandmother
Wallace were never destined to get along under the same
roof because she was from a town family and he from a
country one. For whatever reason, while they never ar-
gued in public, there was much that they disagreed upon
in private.

Still, I was very fond of her. I remember my great
sense of loss and sadness on December 5, 1952 when I was
handed a message as I got off a train. "Fernlake's mother
[Fernlake had been the code name for my mother during
the war] died today at 12:37." As Grandmother wrote in
her letters, I had been her "dear lump of sugar"—and she
had been very much a part of the first twenty-eight years
of my life.

Along with letters from her, there also follow several
letters from another close relative of mine, Mrs. George P.
Wallace. Aunt May was always my favorite aunt. She

called me "tootise" in her letters, and I called her Beufy rhyming with spoofy, because she was always spoofing. My childhood nickname for her clowning somehow stuck.

Dad and I both got along well with Aunt May. She's about eighty-six years old now and still lives right next door to Mother. One of my great pleasures whenever I return to Independence to visit my mother is to also see Aunt May.

Breakfast in the White House, viewed through my camera. Grandmother, Aunt Natalie, Dad.

INDEPENDENCE, MO. TO WASHINGTON, D.C.

January 3, 1938

My dear "Lump of Sugar:"

I have <u>two</u> letters from you today! Both came this A.M.—and they certainly were welcomed—so glad you are getting "fixed up"—and that the apartment is so nice. I wish I could see it all, the new furniture, etc.

What a fine time you are having!—Fred will see about records—and I will send the skates and Dad's shirts and anything else you may want. We all are fine—Just came in after hearing Roosevelt talk—Thought it a splendid one. Of course, you and Mother heard it. We all had a good laugh at David, the night we took down the tree—When we talked about it, he said "Oh! That will be such fun" and, <u>said it several times</u>, while he was wrapping the ornament (which <u>he did beautifully</u>—really). So, after everything was cleaned up and the tree taken out—he stepped over by the south window—and looked for quite a few seconds where the tree had stood—and said—"I sure am mad"—and without another word, walked out of the room. If you could have only seen the expression on his face and the way he walked out.

Tell Mother that Mrs. Woodson died this morning.

I saw Jane "New Year's" Day with Mrs. Merrifield—going toward town.

We had such a nice day—yesterday (Sunday) with Cousin Helen and a lovely dinner. Cousin John and Cousin Marion with little Myra Sue were there too. We were so glad we hadn't gone when you all called. It was so good to hear your voices. Both you and Mums write as often as you can. We miss you all terribly.

Lots and lots of love to all of you, Grandmother

INDEPENDENCE, MO. TO WASHINGTON, D.C. — POSTMARKED
17 FEBRUARY 1941

Monday Morning

My dear "Lump of Sugar":

You were so sweet to send me the dear little Valentine.

I feel that I am an especially favored old lady—with so
many remembrances of the special days—and, you never
forget me.

Thank you my dear—very much—Is Mother very much
"fluffed" up after having the Duke for a dinner partner? We
are all fine this A.M. It is a wonderful morning—just like
Spring. We have the woodpeckers, robins and I heard a rain
crow this morning before I got up.

I am getting so lazy—I hate to move. My ankles are lots
better—and I feel better than I did—but Dr. Allen keeps me
on the medicine.

I wish I had something real newsy to write you dear.

It will seem such a long month until the 22nd of
March. Everyone I see always asks about you and Mother.

Everyone will be glad to see you. It seems queer to see
Uncle Frank walking in and out everyday. He says he
doesn't mind the[?] (It may be my imagination, but I
think he looks better.)

[?] just came in to dust my room, and asked me if I
was writing to you—and asked to thank you for her
Valentine.

Well, I must get dressed. It is almost noon.

Keep well and happy dear.

Lots of love to all,
Grandmother

INDEPENDENCE, MO. TO WASHINGTON, D.C. — POSTMARKED
6 MARCH 1941

My dear "Lump of Sugar":

Just a little letter this time, dear, as I am trying to get some sewing done for little ol' Marion—Everything she has is too short—or worn out.

I called Mrs. Grave to find out about [?] . She said Mrs. O. and Sue were still at the apt. and, until school closes, they will be there—after that they don't know what they will do. Mrs. O. is still in the hospital in the South.

Mr. Graves has a position with the water company and they have moved to 901 N. Liberty Street.

Mrs. Ogen isn't manager at the apt. anymore.

We are all fine. We had a big snow storm last night, but the sun is shining now. Midge Peters told Uncle Frederick last night that Ann was going to Washington Sat. A.M. and they might live there. Lucy said she knew Ann could go out to see you all as soon as she arrived. Everybody is inquiring when you all will be here.

Marion was mad this morning about something—and I called to her several times—she didn't answer, but finally called to say—"I am not talking."

Tell Mother, Uncle George likes his new job, he says. He is the head of the maintenance department for all the county. She (Mother) asked me in her last letter and I forgot to tell her.

Write as often as you can dear.

Love,
Grandmother

INDEPENDENCE, MO. TO WASHINGTON, D.C. — POSTMARKED
13 APRIL 1941

Sunday Morning

My dear "Lump of Sugar":

I am so anxious to see you all—it seems so long since
you left.

No doubt you and Mother are all "dressy up" (as you
used to say, when a little tot) and going to church. C. and F.
have just gone.

I think you are so very sweet to write to me—when my
letters to you have to be so prosy and uninteresting. (Please
excuse all mistakes as Marion is standing here right by
me—asking question after question—and demanding an
answer to every one.)

What are you wearing at the F. M. dance?—and when
do you go? Several of the churches have sunrise services
this morning.

We were so in hopes your father would be able to make
a visit, while so near, hope he comes this week. Write me
about the tea you attended last Sunday dear.

The schools here close in five weeks, Helen Wallace
said.

Wish yours did—so you could come home.

Lots of love dear,
Grandmother

INDEPENDENCE, MO. TO WASHINGTON, D.C. — POSTMARKED
28 NOVEMBER 1941

Friday A.M.

My dear "Lump of Sugar":

I read and read again your good letter. Then the rest of
the family had it to read. They all commented about the fine
chemistry grade.

You and Mother certainly had a "full day" Thanksgiving
—didn't you? It was so fine to talk to you both. It was the first
Thanksgiving you all have not been with us. We certainly
missed you.

I am so glad you enjoyed the[?]. David is going back
to Bryant School.

Monday

I think the child has been so unhappy at the other
school—he dreads going everyday—and doesn't take the
interest he did at Bryant.

Mrs. Allen was here a day or two ago and said Marie
would be home on the 13th of December—Harriet on the
18th. Everyone fine this A.M. and the weather fine too.

We are <u>counting</u> the days now. Will you drive or train?
I've not a thing <u>interesting</u> to write you dear—wish I had
for you are so sweet to write me—Well, I am going to wash
my hair!—so better get at it.

Take care of your dear self.

Lots of love,
Grandmother

INDEPENDENCE, MO. TO WASHINGTON, D.C. — POSTMARKED
12 FEBRUARY 1942

Thursday Evening

My dear "Lump of Sugar":

I am so glad to have yours and Mother's letters this A.M.
I certainly appreciate both as you and Mother are such busy
people these days—it must be hard for you to find time for a
letter.

Marion is much better today—her cold has hung on
longer than the others. Margie, dear, you certainly have
been (so the old darkies used to say) doing yourself proud.
It does not seem to be a bit of trouble for you to stay on that
honor roll.

The contest! I haven't hear that was going on. Tell
me about it. I know it was not any "guessing" work.
Congratulations! dear—which current book did you
choose?

Do you like going to school in the dark? We have had so
much fog in the early morning and all these schoolchildren
look like little shadows going in all directions.

Well, dear, your cake is on its way—do hope it will be
good. Felitta[?] and I got into a heated argument over it so I
let her make it—if it isn't good—write her and tell her.

Uncle "Daw" seems to be getting along all right now.

When you find time, write him a little letter. He was so
glad to have Mother's. I am always ashamed of my letters to
you, dear—for I never know of any interesting news to
write to you.

I am so sorry for the Vaughans.

Do hope he gets his "leave."

Remember me to Virginia.

Write as often as you can—dear.

Love to each one of you dear ones.

Grandmother

INDEPENDENCE, MO. TO WASHINGTON, D.C. — POSTMARKED
15 MARCH 1942

Sunday Morning

My dear "Lump of Sugar:"

You certainly are sweet to write to me when you are so busy with your schoolwork—and your fine grades show your <u>work</u>—we are very <u>proud</u> of you, my dear.

I am glad you feel somewhat comfortable with your "blackouts"—I expect you all hated to see Cal J. leave.

It was a lovely thing for your Glee Club to sing for those poor people. I know it was a little bright spot for them, in their suffering. On which program does Otero sing? I accidentally heard her <u>once</u>—would like to hear her again.

I am glad you can have your chocolate while here—for [?] makes better choc. desserts than others.

I've lost a day this week—consequently I missed sending you or Mother a letter.

<u>We are counting the days until the 28ᵗʰ</u> and <u>they go so slow</u>.

We are all fine!

They are all getting ready for church (C. + F. family).

C. + F. and Aunt Nat and Uncle Frank all went to the city last night to see a basketball game—but a very tame one Uncle Frank thought.

I want C. + F. to mail this for me, so will have to hurry. Both of you write me as often as you can.

Love to each one,
Grandmother

INDEPENDENCE, MO. TO WASHINGTON, D.C. — POSTMARKED
19 MARCH 1942

Thursday afternoon

My dear "Lump of Sugar":

I can't tell you how much I appreciate your good
letters—especially when I have so little of interest to you, to
give you in return.

I am hoping you can have a rest now. That you have
earned such wonderful reports—would love to see the
card—and the rest of the family will want to see it too.

Was [?] as nice as usual? I think the "blackouts" you
are having must be really funny.

Have any of you seen anything of Aunt[?]

I know you and Mother enjoyed your dinner with
Ben. Remember me to her.

Will she remain in Washington? So many of those
offices—are changing around—some to be moved to K.C.
Our chief subject of conversation is "when Bess and Margie
come"—do hope your father is coming too.

Tell me the names of the songs you will have at the
Bazaar.

We are having patches of sunshine today, but a mean
cold wind.

David has lost his first little tooth. Marion came to me
and whispered it to me—and said "Grand Mommie, he looks
so funny"—laughed and said "don't tell him."

C. is going to town so must get this ready to go.

We are counting the days now—they seem too
many—hope the weather will be nice while you are here.

Love—lots of it to all of you dear ones.

Grandmother

INDEPENDENCE, MO. TO WASHINGTON, D.C. — POSTMARKED
9 MAY 1942

Friday Noon

My dear, dear "Lump of Sugar":

Your dear letter came yesterday and I had looked or hoped for it so long—yet I was selfish about it for I know how busy you are all the time and, I am so proud of you dear. You deserve all the good times you have—and I hope you will enjoy the "stars" Thursday night. Your Great-Grandmother had a sweetheart named Hitchcock and I remember so well asking her who the grand looking Army man was (while going though the album one day) and I thought it such a funny name.

I wish I could have seen you in your lovely red dress and coat.

We all want to be there for your graduation and there isn't anything I would not give if I could be—but I am hobbling along and some days not feeling extra well—so, I'll be here dear waiting for you all to come to me.

Tell me all about what you will wear, etc., etc. and do please tell me what I can give you that you would like to have.

David is planning to go to his grandmother's in the City for the weekend—I wish you could look in on Aunt Marg's house—it is going to be nice. However—sometime —but, a mess now. Uncle Daw came home and sat down on the front steps on the porch yesterday—looked so forlorn.

C. is going to town—and will mail this and it's my only chance to get it to the post office.

Write me dear when you can. Will write Mother.

Love to all,
Grandmother

INDEPENDENCE, MO. TO WASHINGTON, D.C.

Monday, September 28, 1942

My dear "Lump of Sugar":

We are <u>so glad</u> to have the telegram this A.M.—and the <u>good news</u> it brought—for as you know, most of us wanted it to be as you decided, but, of course, just where you would be the <u>happiest</u>.

Mrs. S. and I had agreed to call the other whichever received the wire <u>first</u>—so, this morning we were at the phone at the time and said "hello" together—wasn't that strange? We both are <u>very happy</u> about it, dear, and hope you are—and glad the "rush" is over so that you can take a long breath and rest.

Do hope your schoolwork will not be too strenuous, and that you will like it.

Keep well and happy dear—you deserve all the good things that come your way.

Love to all of you dear ones,
Grandmother

Uncle Frank, Aunt May and Aunt Natalie.

DENVER, COLO. TO INDEPENDENCE, MO.—POSTMARKED
19 AUGUST 1944

Saturday Morning

My dear "Lump of Sugar":

I enjoyed your dear letter so much—and while I was impatient for it—I realized your time is so <u>fully</u> taken up with so many other things to do. We noticed in this morning's paper—you and Mother had had sent you by the President and his daughter—<u>a red rose</u>—<u>a very pretty compliment</u> wasn't it?

David and Marion and Joan—Mo's most intimate friend—are going to a children's show this A.M.—so all are up—and D. had his breakfast with F. and I—and during his conversation—he said "Connie" said she didn't like Roosevelt—because he ought not to have had more than <u>two</u> terms. David said—I told her "it was not his fault that he had more—it is the people—they wanted him—so voted for him."

I think I know of the "Toms" and "Joes"—but who is "Ed"? He seems to be quite <u>important</u> too, with the "purple heart," etc.

Well, we had a good time looking at <u>Life</u> yesterday. The pictures! We certainly enjoyed them—and after Frederick called to tell us, he had seen them downtown—and C. said she couldn't wait—and bought one—so I have one of <u>my</u> own.

Ernie and Dick are having dinner with us tomorrow. Dick is being coached in his school work—he missed so much when he had measles.

Well dishes are waiting.

Write as often as you can dear "lump of sugar."

Love—lots of it to all of you
dear ones.
Grandmother

DENVER, COLO. TO INDEPENDENCE, MO.— POSTMARKED
14 SEPTEMBER 1944

Wednesday

My dear "Lump of Sugar":

I was so delighted to have your dear letter letting me
know about all your interesting plans for the Friday of this
week—and your plan for a visit in Columbia. Of course, I'll
be thinking of you Friday—I do that every day—but Friday
will be a special day for us both—and I know we all will be
very proud of you. My dear, as always.

Oh how I want to see your pretty sweaters, dress and
coat—and see them on you. I know how sweet you will look.
Would have given anything to have heard you sing that
beautiful song—Aunt May said in her letter she received
yesterday that you did it so well. Aunt May was so sweet to
go to hear you, wasn't she?

What do you and Mother want for Christmas—and, we
are hoping we will have a house and that all of you will be
with us. Uncle Fred and Christine are planning for that. The
neighbors next door are having dinner with us tonight.
They are always doing something nice for the children or
sending or bringing Christine something so she and
Frederick thought they should do something in return.

Their rock garden has been so beautiful all
summer—and she has kept us in flowers. She brought C. a
jar of chili sauce and one of apple sauce yesterday. C. has
just left with the children for school. Well I had better get
busy—Be sure to write all about what you are doing dear.
We will be all excited and impatient for the record.

Bushels of love dear—to all of you.

Grandmother

P.S. I am shy of paper—hence the one sheet.

DENVER, COLO. TO ?—POSTMARKED 1946 (DATE NOT CLEAR)

My dear "Lump of Sugar":

The <u>lost</u> is <u>found</u> and guess where it was found—<u>right in the bottom of my suitcase</u>. I've just unpacked most of my things—but while getting it all straightened out—getting ready to go home.—C. + F. objected so <u>strenuously</u> about it. I finally put the slips and small things into the dresser drawer <u>last night</u>—and found just what we had a little argument about before I left. I am thoroughly ashamed to send it unlaundered. I wore it for about 10 minutes one day and concluded I was going to <u>burst</u> the seams. So went right back and took it off. I am <u>sure</u>[?]could do a much better job at washing and ironing it. So, sending it to be done there—our Clete isn't the best of ironers—Natalie sent me the clipping I am sending, but no doubt it is <u>old</u> news to you. Will you be <u>another</u> bridesmaid?

We have a real March day, but warm and[?].

Write me dear. I am enclosing Aunt N.'s letter—I too, am sick about the "Queen of the Party."

Love,
Grandmother

? TO ?

May 19, 1947

My precious "Lump of Sugar":

I think you are a very wise little girl and I know it was
very hard for you to decide what to do all by yourself. I am
sure you feel as all of us do, it is best that you wait until you
are happy again. For one cannot sing with sorrow in the
heart and the first concert should be of the best.

May God be with you, my dear, and keep you in your
fine work. I only wish I could see you when you are ready to
go on.

With all the good wishes and my heart full of love.

Grandmother

Lunch under the magnolia tree at the White House.
Counterclockwise: A friend of Mother's, Mrs. Louise Stewart
(don't miss that hat!) Dad, Aunt Natalie, Aunt May, Mother, me,
Grandmother.

INDEPENDENCE, MO. TO ?—POSTMARKED 18 AUGUST 1947

Monday Morning

My precious Margie:

    Just a little note to tell you how terribly I miss you and hoping you are feeling fine! and had a good night's rest.

    I've just written Mother. She called <u>early yesterday</u> morning to ask about your "getting off" and said she was <u>thinking</u> of going to Hollywood. I told her to be <u>sure</u> to <u>go</u>—and I was delighted that she might—do hope she does.

    We are listening for the phone telling us you have arrived safely.

    Keep <u>well</u> and <u>happy</u>.

Bushels of love,
Grandmother

P.S. Remember me to the Stricklers and Mr. Dorsay.

Left to right: Grandmother, Mother, Aunt May, Aunt Natalie, Aunt Mary Jane Truman and Uncle George.

INDEPENDENCE, MO. TO BEVERLY HILLS, CALIF.—
POSTMARKED 20 AUGUST 1947

Wednesday

My precious "Lump of Sugar":

How <u>very sweet</u> you were to write me so soon. I had been dreading the time I would have to wait before I heard—and it is such a dear good letter.

The radio gave us the news of your safe arrival before my or <u>your</u> wire came. I am anxious to hear from Mother this morning to know if she is going to Hollywood.

We are having another one of the awful <u>hot mornings</u> and they promised 102 today, but cooler by night.

I am thinking of you, my dear—much of the time and hoping it is nice and cool there for you and you are feeling <u>well</u> and <u>happy</u>.

Felitta and I keep busy. Yesterday, we put new oilcloth on tables and numerous shelves.

A daily prayer goes for your <u>success</u> and <u>happiness</u> my dear.

Please remember me to Mr. and Mrs. Strickler and Mr. Dorsay.

Love,
Grandmother

INDEPENDENCE, MO. TO BEVERLY HILLS, CALIF. —
POSTMARKED 24 AUGUST 1947

Sunday Morning

My precious "Lump of Sugar":

I can't <u>begin</u> to tell you how <u>proud</u> we are of you! And
wish I could give you a great big <u>hug!</u>

I knew the paper would tell us the wonderful things
you do—the Ovation you had, and all the <u>grand</u> and <u>fine</u>
things that were said about you—<u>my dear.</u>

Do hope you will enjoy the <u>rest</u> of your time there—and
will go to Santa Barbara and Carmel—and other beautiful
places.

Mr. and Mrs. Peters came over last evening—and were
here when we all talked to you. I told them you had talked to
Ann. I'm so glad Ann and[?] could be there—and I'm
glad, too, Miss Jessie called.

Hope you are having a <u>good long rest</u> today—my dear.
You <u>certainly deserve everything you like</u> to "come your
way."

Write me when you can—Margie dear. Mother called
me, this morning—and said, they were "in the clouds" this
morning! They certainly have the <u>greatest appreciation of
what you have accomplished.</u>

Bushels of love, dear with most
sincere congratulations,
Grandmother

INDEPENDENCE, MO. TO MEMPHIS, TENN. — POSTMARKED
12 NOVEMBER 1947

Wednesday

My precious "Lump of Sugar":

You were so dear to send me these lovely pictures of
your dear self. I enjoy taking them out of the envelope and
looking at them, every little while. I am delighted to have
them—all mine—and thank you dear.

And the vases too. So sweet and a kind thought to send
them to me. And if I just could have heard you sing! But, I'm
thinking, every day, "another day near[er]" to your coming
home. All I've seen of "the Club" have raved over your
singing dear and everything else about you—I know you
enjoyed seeing Aunt Nat and Aunt May. They haven't
stopped yet telling me how lovely you were—and sweet you
were, to every one.

I want this letter to go in a hurry to find you. So——

Bushels of love,
Grandmums

Taking a bow after a concert in St. Louis.

INDEPENDENCE, MO. TO TULSA, OKLA. — POSTMARKED
13 NOVEMBER 1947

Thursday

My precious "Lump of Sugar":

 I am thinking of you, my dear (which I do much of the time)—and wishing I knew if you are feeling <u>fine</u>—and getting enough rest. We treasure all the newspaper news and everyone wants the clippings.

 The Little Rock concert was so nice. I liked the nice sincere compliment they gave you, my dear.

 I am rejoicing that this Tulsa one is the last before you go to visit with Mother and Dad and I wish it was to be with <u>me too</u>, but I have to wait about <u>ten days longer</u> for <u>my</u> visit. Oh! but I'll be <u>so glad</u> when you come!

 I'm putting on lace on three of your slips. I have here—save me, all your mending, etc. and bring it with you.

 Do take care of yourself, dear.

 "The Club" said you were <u>wonderful</u> in <u>everything</u>. Write me dear when you can.

Bushels of love and a big hug,
Grandmother

Mrs. George P. Wallace
to Margaret Truman

My grandmother Truman.

INDEPENDENCE, MO. TO WASHINGTON, D.C.—POSTMARKED 8
OCTOBER 1945

Sunday Afternoon

Dear Tootsie:

What a beautiful delicious October day. Went to church
this morning. Came home and listened to the World Series
game, then went for a ride. We went down a road like
"cracker neck" only more so. Wish you all and the Davises
and Rachel could have been along. The country is beautiful
though the leaves have not turned much yet.

> A little drop of ink hadn't seen his big brother for a
> long time, so he asked a big drop of ink what had
> become of him.
> "I thought you knew," he replied in a hushed voice.
> "He's in the pen finishing a sentence." [*Newspaper
> Clipping*]

We all have felt like pricked balloons sine you left and
the excitement died down. It rained and rained and was
cold. A new bunch of S.S.ers have come (Bertram and R [?]
left last Friday—to meet "Poppy" in [?].) They hoped to go
home from there but didn't know, (Barbe + Bubbles Gunn
are just going by for their apt. work.) There are three wives
along this time, but I haven't met any of them yet. They
don't look so hot if you ask me which you didn't.

> Never admit you are fat. Just say you come in the
> large economy size.—*Sagehen*
> A friend is a person who knocks before he enters,
> not after he has left.—*Gargoyle*

There is an all-star program on the radio—so if this
sonds more incoherent than usual (did I stick my neck out
then?) we'll blame it on that. The District attorney is
holding forth now. We read about the wedding in the
paper—was that the debut of the "Rust Smith." Too bad the
weather delayed Pres.—but guess he got to [?] O.K.

Any man can have a wife, but only the iceman can
have his pick.—*Banter*

Did you go shopping in St. Louis or was it too much
trouble to get up? How is Jane? Tell her [?] so Daw and I
are dining alone—Ham loaf, baked sweet potatoes, tomatoes
and choc. ice cream. We are getting down to the [?] you left.
Did the ice cream keep that we put on the train. The train
[?] is going by as usual and every time they slow down, I
think we are having company. Fibber just opened the hall
closet. I cut out the picture of Nelson and found the one of
Clark—so send it too.
Anchors Aweigh is up at the Granala starting today.
Hope to get to see it tho Daw says he isn't interested. Looks
like you all covered most of the front page of the Star this
morning or is that a compliment? Aunt Nat and Uncle
Frank think they are getting off to Denver next Thursday
morning, but I won't believe it until I see them start. We will
be orphans for sure, then, won't we? Maybe we should start
out to go someplace ourselves.
Have you tried out the new cream-colored Ford yet? It
would go nicely with the rust suit. Did your hat ever get
finished? The one to match said suit? I wrote to the family
"at large" last week. So you could take your choice about
who answered or did you ever get it?
Bill has a new P.G. address—N.Y.—so [?] must be going
to Atlanta. Martha Jean didn't lose much time did she.
Meow!!! The ham loaf is about done so I had better wind up
this effusion and finish dinner. Daw is already saying
"Where's my dinner?" He hasn't shaved and dressed all day
so looks like Weary Willie. We put in some of the storm
windows yesterday aft. so he had to rest today. Write when
you have time—if you live through this.

Love,
Beuf

P.S. Instead of a "condemned bridge" on the road today, we
had to ford a creek. We made it.

INDEPENDENCE, MO. TO WASHINGTON, D.C. — POSTMARKED
19 MARCH 1947

Dear Tootsie:

I have been going around in such a dither since Sunday
night. Haven't had sense enough to grasp a pen. This letter
will probably be more or less incoherent, but as one nut to
another?!!! You would have thought your family belonged
to the "Keystone Corps" is you could have seen the
performance we pulled off. It was one night to see, and I use
the word advisedly, with the P's—Daw doesn't have much
opinion of their radio—so we took our small one and tuned
in KCMO at 6:30 to be sure it was G.K. That program came
in fine—no interference at all so we settled down—if you
could call it that—to wait for 7 o'clock. But awoh! awoh! at
seven—a lot of cross talk came on in back and we were all
very unhappy to say the least. When they announced the
orchestra would play a number, I said "Let's dash over and
listen to the other radio at our house." That appealed so we
grabbed our coats and leaped out to the car. It was raining
and Daw was driving so you can imagine the wild ride we
had! Remember, we didn't know the format of the program
and that you might sing right after the first number. We
made it, on two wheels, and jumped out of the car—galloped
into the house and turned the radio on. Breathing a long
sigh of relief, we hear the [?] still on the Irish number.
[?] living room radio—having an aerial and ground cuts
out most of the back talk—so we were all set—and set
we did—when the man started to make a speech, I thought
that Daw would have a nervous breakdown. Then the
orchestra again. Then he started talking about some gal
with a foreign name and Mill almost exploded. He thought
she was going to sing. Then he actually began to introduce
you. I was not nervous—just sorta like hanging suspended
in midair for something to happen. Then, oh boy, did it
happen. I don't think I took three breaths—during the
three songs—and with my build—that is an

accomplishment. You will find, as you get older, how hard it is to say the things you really want to, to the folks you love the most. I expect all the gooey adjectives have been used up by this time. Anyhow—but I know you have known your old Beuf long enough not to need words between us—Nuff said?

Then the telephone began to ring. The K.C. <u>Star</u>: "were we listening to the program?" Asinine! Then folks began to call. Aunt Nat and Uncle Frank were out at Mary and Albert's—and when they came in they said Daw had left the lights burning in his car and the doors open!

Maggie and Maji [?] came out last night and brought the Detroit and New York papers and we had a "jam session" for sure—with "Jersey Cons" for refreshments F. had to go to the ice plant to a directors meeting, but he made record time getting back. Said he will be waiting your <u>check</u> to buy bonds with.

Daw wants to know if you want the Ford in running order when you come in April? It has plenty of antifreeze —so just the battery would have to be put in.

Well, I must close this drivel and get on to mundane accomplishments—Aunt Connie just came in and will mail this for me. Did you see the little poem she wrote about your singing? It's a long way from "The Animal Fair"— and the "Mink à la Mink" to "Charmant Bisean" but let us know when you can come to Independence so we can put on clean sheets.

Love,
Beuf

P.S. You should have seen Spot. Daw told him you were going to sing, so he looked up at the house and then laid down and kept time with his tail.

Miscellaneous Letters

MRS. GEORGE P. WALLACE, INDEPENDENCE, MO., TO HARRY S.
TRUMAN, WASHINGTON, D.C. —POSTMARKED 17 APRIL 1945

Monday Night

Dear Harry:

Gr[?] should I say, "Mr. President"—anyhow I am not
going to. Thanks so much for taking time out of your very
busy day to answer my request, also to write to tell me what
you had done. Of course I did not dream what the week
would bring forth. Neither did you and I suppose it was a
good thing. We could not stand things sometimes if we knew
they were going to happen. My feelings were very divided.
Great sympathy for all of you, to be plunged into such a
maelstrom of events—and abiding faith that you would
know what to do about it.

I am not much of a fatalist, but I do believe that when a
leader is needed, the Good Lord provides one. We have gone
around in a daze since Thurs.—the reaction here is very
gratifying—exploring the theory that "a prophet is not
without honor save in his own country." The consensus of
opinion seems to be that you are the man for the job. As I
stood in my kitchen and heard your opening speech as
President—I thought of all the women and men all over the
country doing the same. It brought back our lovely visit to
Washington in Jan.—and I wished we could have sat in the
"gallery" with Bess and Marg. It seemed to me your
speech was just right—but of course I could be accused of
partiality. We feel like we are so far away and we want to
know so many things. Maybe we will get a letter from
mother tomorrow. We have been pursued by reporters—and
hope we have handled them as you would want us to.

One line from Kipling has been running through my
head. "If you can keep your head while all about you are
losing theirs and blaming it on you"—It takes a pretty solid
foundation, but we Missourians have it. I guess that's
enough to say. Thanks again for bothering with Leonard's
picture. I know he will be thrilled to death. No use telling

you how much George and I wish for you the best of everything. I know you know—or should by this time.

As ever,
May

P.S. Saw your mother Sunday. She looks fine—also Mary J. For heaven sakes—what is the correct way to address the Pres.—don't answer, just rhetorical question.

MRS. GEORGE P. WALLACE, INDEPENDENCE, MO., TO HARRY S.
TRUMAN, WASHINGTON, D.C.—POSTMARKED 10 JUNE 1946

Sunday Afternoon

Dear Harry:

I cut this little "poem" from the St. Louis Post-Dispatch
yesterday on the way home—and think it might give you a
laugh. We had a very pleasant trip home aboard your car
with lots of service and good food. Natalie and George and I
took a ride in St. Louis. The secret service had sent a car,
and Marg and Bess didn't want to. It was nice to move
around a bit as we had almost three hours to kill. We all
slept off and on—and were about thirty minutes late in
getting in as you know. It is quite warm here today, and
doesn't seem possible we were so cold on the boat just a
week ago. We did have such a good time. I think just all
being together and enjoying the beautiful "backyard" and
view of Mr. Jefferson's tomb from the South Portico was as
the main thing. If I'm not careful I will become as lyrical as
our friend Lucy and that would never do!! Thanks again for
a lovely Holiday.

Love,
May

Poem:

TO MRS. TAFT

To the Editor of the "Post-Dispatch"
The Lady Taft says Mr. Truman
Don't Know for sure what he's a-doin',
And what she said of old Missouri
Sounds a lot like Hubby's hooey.
Oh, if someone only knew
Just what to do to tame a shrew.

SKIPPER

Maplewood.

MRS. FRANK WALLACE, INDEPENDENCE, MO., TO HARRY S.
TRUMAN, WASHINGTON, D.C.—POSTMARKED 14 JUNE 1946

Thursday

Dear Harry:

I just wanted to tell you again what a grand time Frank
and I had in D.C. and to thank you for your many
kindnesses to us.

I was glad that Mary was there at the same time, as I
had never known her very well and it gave me a chance to
become better acquainted with her.

I hope you get a break this summer and have some
time to do a few things you want to.

Natalie Ott Wallace

D.W. WALLACE, INDEPENDENCE, MO., TO HARRY S. TRUMAN,
WASHINGTON, D.C.—POSTMARKED 8 SEPTEMBER 1946

Dear Harry:

I do so appreciate your <u>kind thought</u> and <u>beautiful</u>
<u>sweater</u>—<u>thank</u> you many times for it. We are looking
forward to your visit here in the near future.

I hope your Bermuda trip has helped you a lot.
Thanking you <u>again</u>.

> I am most sincerely,
> Madge G. Wallace
> September 7, 1946

MRS. LEE C. HULL, PLATTE CITY, MO., TO MARGARET TRUMAN,
WASHINGTON, D.C.

March 23, 1947

Dear Margaret:

Last Sunday night Oscar and I had a real treat listening to
you sing. It sounded wonderful to us and we both feel an
immense pride in our little cousin. Do you mind my calling
you that? You seem so young to us and because of that your
accomplishment is all the greater. I also was most
interested in the comments of the critics. Weren't you on
the whole much pleased? I was particularly interested in
one who spoke of the richness of tone in the middle scale,
because it was that, as I listened to you, that came to me as
being one of the qualities that you added to all that was good
before when I had heard your records or the few times that
I had heard you sing. I am very far from being a music
critic, but I am sure that you are off to a tremendous start.

We are all well. Wills is busy with track now. His studies are
of course a secondary matter. He has grown a lot, is about
five ten and a half tall now. Pete is still near Tokyo. He
writes that he will see me in ten months.

Oscar and I send our love and congratulations to you in
your outstanding achievement.

Affectionately,
Louise

I do regret that I have no letters to include here from one who played such an important role in history, the woman who brought Dad up, my Grandmother Truman. (Yes, the same one who was so widely quoted when asked if she wasn't proud of her son Harry, who had just become President of the United States. "Of course I'm proud of him," Mamma Truman snapped. "But I have other children I'm just as proud of. I have a daughter and another son who are just as fine as Harry.")

It was perhaps from Mamma Truman that Dad got his sense of history, for her long life span encompassed so much that was important in our country's life. She was born when America had less than 25 million people and Millard Fillmore was President. She witnessed the raiding parties of the Civil War, two world wars, and lived long enough to see her son become President of the United States of America.

Although around Mamma Truman the whole world changed, Mamma Truman did not. Her philosophy never altered, and it was simply that you should know right from wrong, you should always try to do what's right, and you should always try to do your best. She taught that lesson to her son, he tried to teach it to me, and he also tried to teach it to our country.

ABOUT THE AUTHOR:

Margaret Truman is a lecturer and author of, among others, *Souvenir, Women of Courage*; the bestselling biography of her father, *Harry S. Truman*; and the novels *Murder in the White House* and *Murder on Capitol Hill*.

Born in Independence, Mo., she now makes her home in New York City. She is married to Clifton Daniel and has four sons.